SAP R/3 Transaction Codes: SAP R3 and SAP ECC Transaction Code Review for SAP MM, SAP SD, SAP FICO, and Netweaver

SAP R/3 Transaction Codes: SAP R3 and SAP ECC
Transaction Code Review for SAP MM, SAP SD, SAP FICO,
and Netweaver

ISBN: 978-1-60332-012-2

Edited By: Jamie Fisher

Printed in the United States of America

Please visit our website at www.sapcookbook.com

Table of Contents

Introduction: Finding the list of SAP Transaction codes

Question: Where can I find the list of transaction codes and their usage? I heard that there is some table which contains all the transaction codes with their descriptions.
Does anyone know about the Table that consist all the T-Code?

A: Listed here are the various ways you can find the list of transaction codes and their usage:
Use transaction **SE11 - ABAP Dictionary**:
Fill in the Database table name and click the Display button.
- TSTC table will contain all the Tcodes and
- TSTCT table will contain all the Tcodes with Texts.
Once you entered the screen, click in Top Menu - Utilities - Table contents - Display
If you want to display all the transaction code (total - 57,048) you have to change the Fields: Maximum number of hits to 99999 (default 500).
Or
Simply go to transaction **SM01**, although this tcode is to Lock/Unlock any transaction code, you can also view all the tcode available in the R/3 system from here.
Or
Go to transaction **SE93**
There are two ways where you can find the list of transaction codes in **SE93**.

Method 1:
You must be familiar with the starting characters strings for each of the R/3 application modules.
Assuming you know that most Materials Management transaction codes start with MM.
In the Fields: Transaction code, type in MM* and press the function key F4
The list of transaction code starting with MM will be displayed.

Method 2:
On the Top Menu, click Utilities - Find - Execute and the first 500 transaction will be display.

If want to display all the tcodes, make sure you remembered to change the Fields: Maximum no. of hits right at the bottom of the screen.

Question: I know a particular T Code and can enter and work on it. How do I know what is the menu path for that T Code?

A: Enter Search_SAP_Menu in the command box and when the pop box appears enter, the Tcode and it will give the nodes and menu path.

This is helpful only in case of SAP Menu not in case of SPRO - i.e. IMG.

Quick Reference Guide to Basic Transaction Codes

Editing Preferences	**FB00**
Initiate and Complete a Journal Entry Document	**F-65**
Monitor Status of Completed Documents via SAP Business Workplace (Initiator's Outbox)	**SBWP**
Change a Parked Document	**FBV2**
Display Changes to a Parked Document	**FBV5**
Display a Parked Document	**FBV3**
Delete a Parked Document	**FBV0**
Create an Account Assignment Model	**FKMT**
Change or Delete an Account Assignment Model	**FKMT**
Excel JV Upload	**ZF104**
Approve or Reject Completed Documents (Approver's Inbox)	**SBWP**
Forward a Completed Document to Another Approver	**SBWP**
Create, View, and Change Attachments (Inbox)	**SBWP**
Display a Posted Journal Entry	**FB03**
Change a Posted Journal Entry	**FB02**
Display Changes to a Posted Journal Entry	**FB04**

Report to Track Journal Entries Awaiting Approval	ZF180
Report to Track Non-Posted Journal Entries	ZF182
Report to Track Posted Journal Entries	ZF181

SAP R/3 T-Codes for MM

Question 01: Create a movement type

How do you create a movement type? When will movement type numbers be odd?

A: When prompted by a dialog box after an activity, you copy a movement type. Select the field "Movement Type" and "Continue". In the Define Work area, enter the movement type to be copied in *"From:"* and the name your new movement type in the *"To:"* field. Now choose *"Continue"*. Choose the desired movement type you want then choose *"Edit → Copy as"* and re-type the selected movement type with the new type copy all dependent entries and make sure to begin with a proper prefix (9,X,Z). All control indicators are copied to the new movement type. Review the new movement type changing any necessary controls. Reversal movement types are numbered as the number type plus one. The reversal for movement type 451 (Returns From Customer) is 452. As a last step before saving your settings, add a copy the reversal movement type and enter it in *Reversal/follow-on movement types.*

Question 02: Adopt standard settings for message determination

How do you adopt standard settings for the Message Determination Facility in MM-PUR?

A: The Message Determination Facility is by default active and message determination schema is supplied for all purchasing documents including POs, PRs, RFQs etc.

All of the desired message types must be maintained. Choose Master data → Messages → Purchasing document → Create or Change from the Purchasing menu. Add the message type and pick the key combination. The key combination decides the condition table where the condition record is stored. Enter all needed items. Next screen, create the individual condition records. Using the menu options Goto → Means of Communication, enter the proper peripheral, or output for each message record. Save.

Question 03: Set price control for receipts

How do you set price control for receipts (goods/invoice) telling the system how to value stocks?

A: Transaction Code OMW1 allows you to set price control to S (Standard Price) or V (Moving Average Price).

Under Standard Price (S), the materials and accounting documents are both valid. The one with the lower value will be posted with a price variance entry.

Question 04: Accessing Materials Management Configuration Menu

How do you access the Materials Management Configuration Menu?

A: Transaction Code OLMS has a host of options that are not accessible through the IMG.

Question 05: Access to MM configuration transactions

How are the various MM configuration Transactions accessed?

A: Transaction Codes OLMD accesses MM-CBP, OLMB accesses MM-IM, OLME accesses MM-PUR, OLML accesses MM-Warehouse Management, OLMS accesses Material Master Data, and OLMW is the proper transaction for valuation and account assignment.

Question 06: Important Materials Management Tables

What are some of the more important Materials Management Tables?

A: EINA contains general data of the (Purchasing) Information Record; EINE includes Purchasing Organization of the same. MAKT is the Materials Description table, MARA-General Materials data, MARC-Plant Data for Materials, MARD-Storage Location Data for Material, MAST-Material to BOM Link, MBEW-Material Valuation, and MKPF-Header Material Document.

Some of the tables that directly pertain to the document types are T156 Movement Type and T023/T024 Groups Material and Purchasing.

Question 07: Add custom fields to POs and RFQs

Can you add custom fields to POs and RFQs?

A: Yes, you can. You can add custom fields to the customer including structures I_EKKODB and I_EKPODB.
Create a project via CMOD for enhancement MM06E005. Follow the documentation for MM06E005, and create the sub-screens for function group XM06 using transaction SE80. Add fields to the appropriate screen. It is recommended that you call the screen fields EKPO_CI-name or EKKO_CI-name. This simplifies transferring data to/from the screen. Put code in EXIT_SAPMM06E_018 to transfer data from sub-screen to structure E_CI_EKPO. Put code in EXIT_SAPMM06E_016 to transfer data from database to sub-screen using structure I_CI_EKPO. In the PBO of the sub-screen, do any processing to make fields display only, or hide them. If you need values from the main screen to make decisions in the sub-screen, define variables in the global data part of the function module, and fill the variables in EXIT_SAPMM06E_016 (PBO of main screen) Make sure everything has been activated like user exists, screens, etc.

Question 08: Dictate Planned Orders conversions

Where can you dictate how Planned Orders are converted into Requisitions in MRP?

A: Look at the Transaction Code OPPR indicator. Assign the proper indicator.

Question 09: Update or create Material Master Records

What SAP program is used to update or create Material Master Records?

A: RMDATIND is used to update Material Master Records and can be used for such assignments as extending all materials to a new plant.

Question 10: Materials Views

What Views are possible for a material?

A: The material type selected controls the views possible for material.

For a material to be used in the system it needs to be created for each plant. Multiple views of a material are possible but at a minimum, the material needs to have a description and a base unit of measure assigned on the basic data view. Additional department views (i.e. Accounting, Sales, Purchasing, MRP, Warehouse) can be added at a later time by extending the material. As additional plants are added, a material will need to be extended to the plants before it can be used there.

Question 11: Production Resource/Tool defined as a material

When can a Production Resource/Tool be defined as a material?

A: A Production Resource / Tool can be defined as a material if purchasing and inventory functions are to be carried out for that PRT.

The information required to be input is dependent upon which department views are being created. Thus, material master information is typically entered at different times by numerous system users. Note that to add a view, the "Create Material" transaction is used rather than the "Change Material" transaction.

Question 12: Creating a new Material

When creating a new Material, what may prompt some of the possible Material Types?

A: Pressing F4 gives a list of choices. Select the material type for the material you are creating. Examples of these are FHMI for Production, Resources/tools, ROH for Raw Materials, and FERT for Finished Products, etc.

Question 13: Materials Views perspective

How do you determine which views of a material need to be added or to see which plants a material has been extended to?

A: You can use transaction MM50.

To extend a material to a different plant requires selecting the new plant on the organizational level screen. Note that all views of a material are not extended unless they were selected on the initial screen. In addition, each plant may have a different system configuration requiring additional inputs on each of the departmental screens. Material changes made in one plant do not change that material in other plants.

Question 14: Set user defaults for views and organizational levels

How can you set user defaults for views and organizational levels?

A: The user defaults for views can be set under Menus: Defaults → Views. Select those views to be checked on by default when generating a new material. Select 'View selection only on request' option when the select view pop-up is to be by-passed.

For organizational levels, Menus: Defaults → organizational levels. Enter those organizational levels to be defaulted when generating a new material. Select 'Org. levels/profiles only on request' when the select view pop-up is to be by-passed unless selected.

Question 15: Requisites for automatic copy

What needs to be present in order for Material Type to be automatically copied from one view to another?

A: When creating any view, the Industry Sector and Material type will be automatically copied from an existing view, so long as at least one view exists.

Question 16: Create a document/e-mail notifier

How do you create a document/e-mail notifying your supplier or internal personnel when an invoice plan is settled?

A: The IMG setting is Material Management → Logistics Invoice Verification → Message Determination.

If these settings are not made, the message "Invoicing Plan: No Message Was Found for Partner XXX, Company Code XXX". If the notifying documents are not required, simply turn off the message by changing the message from "error" to "information" using Material Management → Logistic Invoice Verification → Define Attributes of System Messages.

Question 17: Authority settings

How can one keep users from using standard MM Movement Types?

A: Standard Movement Types should not be deleted from the system. The account assignments, however, may be deleted for a particular Movement Type in table T030 using transaction OBYC.

Another way to achieve the same result is to enter Movement Type in transaction OMJJ. Remove MBXX from allowed transactions.

Question 18: Define a Release Procedure for PRs and POs

How do you define a Release Procedure for PRs and POs?

A: Use Transaction ME54 and ME28 respectively.

Question 19: Change Characteristic

How do you accomplish and do the "Change Characteristic"?

A: Use Transaction Code CT04. Follow these steps: Format (numeric, character, etc.), Unit of Measure, Templates, Required Entry, Intervals as Values , descriptions for texts for characteristics and characteristic values, display options for characteristics on the value assignment screen, Allowed Values, Default Values that are set automatically on the Value Assignment Screen.

Question 20: Create a Class

How do you create a Class?

A: Class is defined as the group of characteristics, which can be attributed to a product. Use Transaction CL01. Enter the value for the Class name and a small description. Select the group from it. The values on the different tabs are not mandatory, so you can skip the values if you wish or you can go to any extent needed. Save, and the Class is created.

Question 21: Configure the Release Procedure

How do you configure the Release Procedure?

A: Use Transaction OMGQ.

Question 22: Sales and Purchasing view

Will ROH have a sales view? Will FERT have a purchasing view?

A: They shouldn't because ROH type materials are procured from the outside not sold and FERT type materials are created inside and aren't procured.

In some special cases, we have to sell raw materials (ROH) and buy finished goods (FERT) from outside sources. The views must be extended in these cases using transactions OMS2 and MM50.

Question 23: Create Vendor Account Groups

Where do we create Vendor Account Groups, or screen layout in Vendor Master?

A: Using SPRO, go to Financial Accounting → Accounts Payable/Receivable → Vendor Accounts → Master Records → Preparations for Creating Vendor Master Records → define Account Groups With Screen Layout (Vendors) or define Screen Layout Per Activity.

Question 24: Material Master Key Fields

What are the key fields for the Material Master?

A: The key fields are: Material Groups, External Material Groups, Divisions, Material Status, Labs & Offices, Basic Materials, Storage Conditions, Temperature Conditions, Container Requirements, and Units or Measure Groups.

Question 25: Main Purchasing Tables

What are the main Purchasing Tables?

A: These are the main purchasing tables:

-EKBN   Purchase Requisition
-EBKN Purchase Requisition Account Assignment
-EKAB   Release Documentation
-EKBE   History of Purchase Document

Question 26: Create a material

How do you create a material?

A: Use Transaction Code MM01. Name the material, choose an industry sector, choose a material type, create or copy the views, add a basic description, give it's attributes/values, MRP information, reorder point, accounting valuation, warehouse management information and then save the data.

Question 27: Data points provided by Purchasing for a material

What are some of the data points provided by Purchasing for a material?

A: Some of the key inputs when creating a material are Base Unit of Measure, Purchasing Group, Reminder days, tolerance levels, shipping instructions, GR processing time, JIT schedule indicator, Critical part, etc.

Question 28: Lot Size attributes of a material

What is the Lot Size attributes a material can posse?

A: Lot Sizing dictates the reorder quantity for a material. A material can have a static, periodic, optimum, or fixed lot size.

Question 29: Create a Vendor

How do you create a Vendor?

A: Use Transaction Code XK01. Add the Vendor name, Company Code, Purchasing Organization, Account Group, and the Vendor address. Next add the country, Bank Key, Bank Account, Account Holder (an actual name), and then save the data.

Question 30: materials assigned to vendors

How are materials assigned to vendors?

A: Information Record links materials to the vendor, thus facilitating the process of selecting quotations. Use Transaction Code ME11 or Logistics → Material Management → Purchasing and then Master Data → Info Record → Create.

Question 31: Information Record Data contents

What data does the Information Record contain?

A: The Information Record has data on Units of Measure, Vendor price changes after a certain level, what materials have been procured by a specific vendor, price and conditions for relevant Purchase Organization, Tolerance limits for over/under delivery, Vendor evaluation data, planned delivery time, and availability time the vendor can supply the material.

Question 32: Create the Information Record

How do you create the Information Record based on the Material Master record?

A: In the IMG, Master Data → Info Record → Create. Enter Vendor Number, Material Number, Purchasing Organization or Plant Number. Enter the number of the Information Record if external number assignments are used (left blank, the system will assign a number). Enter the General Data for the Vendor, order unit, origin data, and supply option, Customs Tariff Number. Next, enter the Vendor's planned delivery time (used for scheduling), responsible Purchasing Group, and Standard PO quantity (used in conjunction with price scales for price determination). Check the Control Data. The tolerance data and the responsible purchasing group are taken as default values from the Material Master record. Enter the net price. Now, from the top of the screen go to → Texts to display the text overview. You can enter the info memo or the PO text. If the PO text is already defined in the Material Master record, it appears as a default value. Save the record.

Question 33: Initial configuration steps for Purchase Requisitions

What are some of the initial configuration steps for Purchase Requisitions?

A: Define Document Types, Processing Time, Release Procedure (with and without classification), Setup Authorization Check for G/L Accounts, Define Number Range.

Question 34: Setup Stock Transport Order

When, in initial configuration, why would you have to Setup Stock Transport Order?

A: If it is required to carry out an inter-plant Stock Transfer through SD, then this configuration is required and must be carried out.

Question 35: Initial configuration steps for Inventory Management

What are some of the initial configuration steps for Inventory Management?

A: Go to Plant Parameters, Define System Message Attributes, Number Assignment (Allocate document type FI to transactions), Goods Issues, Transfer Postings, Define Screen Layout, maintain Copy Rules for Reference Documents, Setup Dynamic Availability Check, Allow Negative Stocks.

Define Default Values for Physical Inventory Document, Batch Input Reports, Tolerances for Physical Inventory Differences, and Inventory Sampling. Cycle Counting should be configured as well.

Complete MM Transaction Codes List

ME01	Maintain Source List
ME03	Display Source List
ME04	Changes to Source List
ME05	Generate Source List
ME06	Analyze Source List
ME07	Reorganize Source List
ME08	Send Source List
ME0M	Source List for Material
ME11	Create Purchasing Info Record
ME12	Change Purchasing Info Record
ME13	Display Purchasing Info Record
ME14	Changes to Purchasing Info Record
ME15	Flag Purchase Info Rec. for Deletion
ME16	Purchasing Info Recs. for Deletion
ME17	Archive Info Records
ME18	Send Purchasing Info Record
ME1A	Archived Purchasing Info Records
ME1B	Re-determine Info Record Price
ME1E	Quotation Price History
ME1L	Info Records Per Vendor
ME1M	Info Records per Material
ME1P	Purchase Order Price History
ME1W	Info Records Per Material Group
ME1X	Buyer's Negotiation Sheet for Vendor
ME1Y	Buyer's Negotiation Sheet for Material
ME21	Create Purchase Order
ME21N	Create Purchase Order
ME22	Change Purchase Order
ME22N	Change Purchase Order
ME23	Display Purchase Order
ME23N	Display Purchase Order
ME24	Maintain Purchase Order Supplement
ME25	Create PO with Source Determination
ME26	Display PO Supplement (IR)
ME27	Create Stock Transport Order
ME28	Release Purchase Order
ME29N	Release purchase order
ME2A	Monitor Confirmations
ME2B	POs by Requirement Tracking Number
ME2C	Purchase Orders by Material Group
ME2J	Purchase Orders for Project

ME2K	Purchase Orders by Account Assignment
ME2L	Purchase Orders by Vendor
ME2M	Purchase Orders by Material
ME2N	Purchase Orders by PO Number
ME2O	SC Stock Monitoring (Vendor)
ME2S	Services per Purchase Order
ME2V	Goods Receipt Forecast
ME2W	Purchase Orders for Supplying Plant
ME308	Send Contracts with Conditions
ME31	Create Outline Agreement
ME31K	Create Contract
ME31L	Create Scheduling Agreement
ME32	Change Outline Agreement
ME32K	Change Contract
ME32L	Change Scheduling Agreement
ME33	Display Outline Agreement
ME33K	Display Contract
ME33L	Display Scheduling Agreement
ME34	Maintain Outline Agreement Supplement
ME34K	Maintain Contract Supplement
ME34L	Maintain Scheduled Agreement Supplement
ME35	Release Outline Agreement
ME35K	Release Contract
ME35L	Release Scheduling Agreement
ME36	Display Agreement Supplement (IR)
ME37	Create Transport Scheduling Agreement
ME38	Maintain Scheduled Agreement Schedule
ME39	Display Scheduled Agreement. Schedule (TEST)
ME3A	Transmit Release Documentation Record
ME3B	Outline Agreements per Requirement Number
ME3C	Outline Agreements by Material Group
ME3J	Outline Agreements per Project
ME3K	Outline Agreements by Acct. Assignment
ME3L	Outline Agreements per Vendor
ME3M	Outline Agreements by Material
ME3N	Outline Agreements by Agreement Number
ME3P	Recalculate Contract Price
ME3R	Recalculate Scheduled Agreement Price
ME3S	Service List for Contract
ME41	Create Request For Quotation
ME42	Change Request For Quotation
ME43	Display Request For Quotation
ME44	Maintain RFQ Supplement
ME45	Release RFQ

ME47	Create Quotation
ME48	Display Quotation
ME49	Price Comparison List
ME4B	RFQs by Requirement Tracking Number
ME4C	RFQs by Material Group
ME4L	RFQs by Vendor
ME4M	RFQs by Material
ME4N	RFQs by RFQ Number
ME4S	RFQs by Collective Number
ME51	Create Purchase Requisition
ME51N	Create Purchase Requisition
ME52	Change Purchase Requisition
ME52N	Change Purchase Requisition
ME52NB	Buyer Approval: Purchase Requisition
ME53	Display Purchase Requisition
ME53N	Display Purchase Requisition
ME54	Release Purchase Requisition
ME54N	Release Purchase Requisition
ME55	Collective Release of Purchase Requirements
ME56	Assign Source to Purchase Requisition
ME57	Assign and Process Requisitions
ME58	Ordering: Assigned Requisitions
ME59	Automatic Generation of POs
ME59N	Automatic generation of POs
ME5A	Purchase Requisitions: List Display
ME5F	Release Reminder: Purchase Requisition
ME5J	Purchase Requisitions for Project
ME5K	Requisitions by Account Assignment
ME5R	Archived Purchase Requisitions
ME5W	Resubmission of Purchase Requisitions
ME61	Maintain Vendor Evaluation
ME62	Display Vendor Evaluation
ME63	Evaluation of Automatic Sub criteria
ME64	Evaluation Comparison
ME65	Evaluation Lists
ME6A	Changes to Vendor Evaluation
ME6B	Display Vendor Evaluation for Material
ME6C	Vendors without Evaluation
ME6D	Vendors Not Evaluated Since...
ME6E	Evaluation Records without Weighting
ME6F	Print
ME6G	Vendor Evaluation in the Background
ME6H	Standard Analysis: Vendor Evaluation
ME6Z	Transport Vendor Evaluation Tables

ME80	Purchasing Reporting
ME80A	Purchasing Reporting: RFQs
ME80AN	General Analyses (A)
ME80F	Purchasing Reporting: POs
ME80FN	General Analyses (F)
ME80R	Purchasing Reporting: Outline Agreements.
ME80RN	General Analyses (L,K)
ME81	Analysis of Order Values
ME81N	Analysis of Order Values
ME82	Archived Purchasing Documents
ME84	Generation of Scheduled Agreement Releases
ME84A	Individual Display of SA Release
ME85	Renumber Schedule Lines
ME86	Aggregate Schedule Lines
ME87	Aggregate PO History
ME88	Set Agreement Cum. Qty./Reconciliation Date
ME91	Purchasing Documents: Urging/Reminding
ME91A	Urge Submission of Quotations
ME91E	Scheduled Agreement. Schedules: Urging/Remind.
ME91F	Purchase Orders: Urging/Reminders
ME92	Monitor Order Acknowledgment
ME92F	Monitor Order Acknowledgment
ME92K	Monitor Order Acknowledgment
ME92L	Monitor Order Acknowledgment
ME97	Archive Purchase Requisitions
ME98	Archive Purchasing Documents
ME99	Messages from Purchase Orders
ME9A	Message Output: RFQs
ME9E	Message Output: Scheduled Agreement Schedules
ME9F	Message Output: Purchase Orders
ME9K	Message Output: Contracts
ME9L	Message Output: Scheduled Agreements
MEAN	Delivery Addresses
MEB0	Reversal of Settlement Runs
MEB1	Create Reb. Arrangs. (Subseq. Sett.)
MEB2	Change Reb. Arrangs. (Subseq. Sett.)
MEB3	Displ. Reb. Arrangs. (Subseq. Sett.)
MEB4	Settlement re Vendor Rebate Arrs.
MEB5	List of Vendor Rebate Arrangements
MEB6	Busn. Vol. Data, Vendor Rebate Arrs.
MEB7	Extend Vendor Rebate Arrangements
MEB8	Det. Statement, Vendor Rebate Arrs.
MEB9	Stat. Statement, Vendor Rebate Arrs.
MEBA	Comp. Suppl. BV, Vendor Rebate Arr.

MEBB	Check Open Docs., Vendor Reb. Arrs.
MEBC	Check Customizing: Subsequent Sett.
MEBE	Workflow Sett. re Vendor Reb. Arrs.
MEBF	Updating of External Busn. Volumes
MEBG	Chg. Curr. (Euro), Vend. Reb. Arrs.
MEBH	Generate Work Items (Man. Extension)
MEBI	Message, Subs.Settlem. - Settlem.Run
MEBJ	Recompile Income, Vendor Reb. Arrs.
MEBK	Message., Subs. Settlem.- Arrangment
MEBM	List of settlement runs for arrngmts
MEBR	Archive Rebate Arrangements
MEBS	Stmnt. Sett. Docs., Vend. Reb. Arrs.
MEBT	Test Data: External Business Volumes
MEBV	Extend Rebate Arrangements (Dialog)
MECCP_ME2K	For Requisition Account Assignment
MEDL	Price Change: Contract
MEI1	Automatic Purchasing Document Change
MEI2	Automatic Document Change
MEI3	Recompilation of Document Index
MEI4	Compile Worklist for Document Index
MEI5	Delete Worklist for Document Index
MEI6	Delete purchasing document index
MEI7	Change sales prices in purch. orders
MEI8	Recomp. doc. index settlement req.
MEI9	Recomp. doc. index vendor bill. doc.
MEIA	New Structure Doc.Ind. Cust. Sett.
MEIS	Data Selection: Arrivals
MEK1	Create Conditions (Purchasing)
MEK2	Change Conditions (Purchasing)
MEK3	Display Conditions (Purchasing)
MEK31	Condition Maintenance: Change
MEK32	Condition Maintenance: Change
MEK33	Condition Maintenance: Change
MEK4	Create Conditions (Purchasing)
MEKA	Conditions: General Overview
MEKB	Conditions by Contract
MEKC	Conditions by Info Record
MEKD	Conditions for Material Group
MEKE	Conditions for Vendor
MEKF	Conditions for Material Type
MEKG	Conditions for Condition Group
MEKH	Market Price
MEKI	Conditions for Incoterms
MEKJ	Conditions for Invoicing Party

MEKK	Conditions for Vendor Sub-Range
MEKL	Price Change: Scheduling Agreements
MEKLE	Currency Change: Sched. Agreements
MEKP	Price Change: Info Records
MEKPE	Currency Change: Info Records
MEKR	Price Change: Contracts
MEKRE	Currency Change: Contracts
MEKX	Transport Condition Types Purchasing
MEKY	Trnsp. Calc. Schema: Mkt. Pr. (Pur.)
MEKZ	Trnsp. Calculation Schemas (Purch.)
MELB	Purch. Transactions by Tracking No.
MEMASSIN	Mass-Changing of Purch. Info Records
MEMASSPO	Mass Change of Purchase Orders
MEMASSRQ	Mass-Changing of Purch. Requisitions
MENU_MIGRATION	Menu Migration into New Hierarchy
MEPA	Order Price Simulation/Price Info
MEPB	Price Info/Vendor Negotiations
MEPO	Purchase Order
MEQ1	Maintain Quota Arrangement
MEQ3	Display Quota Arrangement
MEQ4	Changes to Quota Arrangement
MEQ6	Analyze Quota Arrangement
MEQ7	Reorganize Quota Arrangement
MEQ8	Monitor Quota Arrangements
MEQB	Revise Quota Arrangement
MEQM	Quota Arrangement for Material
MER4	Settlement re Customer Rebate Arrs.
MER5	List of Customer Rebate Arrangements
MER6	Busn. Vols., Cust. Reb. Arrangements
MER7	Extension of Cust. Reb. Arrangements
MER8	Det. Statement: Cust. Rebate Arrs.
MER9	Statement: Customer Reb. Arr. Stats.
MERA	Comp. Suppl. BV, Cust. Rebate Arrs.
MERB	Check re Open Docs. Cust. Reb. Arr.
MERE	Workflow: Sett. Cust. Rebate Arrs.
MEREP_EX_REPLIC	SAP Mobile: Execute Replicator
MEREP_GROUP	SAP Mobile: Mobile Group
MEREP_LOG	SAP Mobile: Activity Log
MEREP_MIG	SAP Mobile: Migration
MEREP_MON	SAP Mobile: Mobile Monitor
MEREP_PD	SAP Mobile: Profile Dialog
MEREP_PURGE	SAP Mobile: Purge Tool
MEREP_SBUILDER	SAP Mobile: SyncBO Builder
MEREP_SCENGEN	SAP Mobile: SyncBO Generator

MERF	Updating of External Busn. Volumes
MERG	Change Curr. (Euro) Cust. Reb. Arrs.
MERH	Generate Work Items (Man. Extension)
MERJ	Recomp. of Income, Cust. Reb. Arrs.
MERS	Stmnt. Sett. Docs. Cust. Reb. Arrs.
MEU0	Assign User to User Group
MEU2	Perform Busn. Volume Comp.: Rebate
MEU3	Display Busn. Volume Comp.: Rebate
MEU4	Display Busn. Volume Comp.: Rebate
MEU5	Display Busn. Volume Comp.: Rebate
MEW0	Procurement Transaction
MEW1	Create Requirement Request
MEW10	Service Entry in Web
MEW2	Status Display: Requirement Requests
MEW3	Collective Release of Purchase Reqs.
MEW5	Collective Release of Purchase Order
MEW6	Assign Purchase Orders WEB
MEW7	Release of Service Entry Sheets
MEW8	Release of Service Entry Sheet
MEW9	mew9
MEWP	Web based PO
MEWS	Service Entry (Component)
ME_SWP_ALERT	Display MRP Alerts (Web)
ME_SWP_CO	Display Purchasing Pricing (Web)
ME_SWP_IV	Display Settlement Status (Web)
ME_SWP_PDI	Display Purchase Document Info (Web)
ME_SWP_PH	Display Purchasing History (Web)
ME_SWP_SRI	Display Schedule Releases (Web)
ME_WIZARD	ME: Registration and Generation

SAP R/3 Transaction codes for HR

Info Types

Question 01: Configuring a custom feature for a default contract type

I have made a custom feature to default the contract type in info type 0001. Since it is a custom feature, it needs to be linked somewhere to that field to default the value.

If there is some USER EXIT which one should I use?

What is the command to call a feature?

A: There is user exit within enhancement PBAS0001 that may be used to assign default values in all info types. You can also use the zxpadu01 or 02 user exits.

Question 02: Info type 0019, Monitoring of Tasks

We are tracking employees on Sabbatical Leave using IT-0019. When an employee goes on a 'Sabbatical leave', we create an action that calls IT-0000, IT-0001, and IT-0019. IT-0019 is used to record the expected return date and set up a reminder. If the employee does not return but is extended, we create another IT-0019 using PA30 with the new expected return date and a new reminder.

When the employee finally returns, we create an action that calls IT-000, IT-0001, and IT-0019 in the background via a dynamic action. The dynamic action should set the monitoring date to 2-task completed.

This is working fine except for those records that have multiple IT-0019 (extensions).

Is there a way to make the dynamic action mark all IT-0019, Subtype 13's as 2-task completed and not just the last one?

My dynamic action looks like the following:

```
0000 04 66 P P0000-MASSG='SR'
0000 04 67 I MOD,19,13,,/D
0000 04 68 W P0019-BVMRK='2'
```

A: You can set it to two (2) via a function module. With dynamic actions, you do not loop over all the records you want to modify. You should find one and modify it.

Question 03: Tracking viewed info types

Transaction S_AHR_61016380 can be used to track changes to infotypes as set in the V_T585A table. This is a good tool for tracking updates, deletes and changes.

Is there a means to track viewed infotypes?

A: I don't think there's a standard solution. There is, however, an object history that if switched on, it can tell you the last few personnel numbers looked at. But there's no certainty that this is configurable by basis to show more details.

Another method is to use a user exit to trigger an update to a customer table storing the user name, time, etc.

You can also try to consult your basis consultant regarding "System Trace". At OS level, system records which the user has executed shows which transaction and when.

Question 04: Storing federal tax id with the SSN

In our business, we treat some contract employees as independent business entities. So, we need to store their federal tax id along with the SSN on an employee record.

Is there any way in SAP that this can be achieved?

A: You have to give the Infotype permissibility to the country code you are using. E.g. If you are using MOLGA IS 40, Indian country code, then you have to go to the node:

SPRO --> Personnel Management --> Personnel Administration --> Customizing Procedures --> Infotypes--> Assign Infotypes to countries

Now, select one line (any line) --> copy --> and accordingly you change it for your requirement.

E.g. Give the IT (0185) and the Sub type (if you have any specific, or just leave it blank), and then give the country code, and select the 'Push' button, Permitted --> SAVE

By doing this, you are assigning or giving the permissibility to your country code to use this Info type.

Then, come out of the screen and go to PA30, you will be able to use IT 0185.

Question 05: Applicant group

One of our customers would like to be able to group an applicant by more than one applicant group. They want to group their applicants by the types of jobs in their company. Many applicants are interested in more than one job type, and would therefore be grouped in two or even more groups. I was wondering whether we might have to create a customer infotype to store this information or maybe use the qualifications catalogue.

Is there a way to group an applicant in more than one applicant group?

Or are there some other groupings we can use to store this information?

A: It seems like you are using the old 'SAP Recruitment'. But in E-Recruiting, there is a new PD object "Job Family coming out in an upcoming support pack that looks like what you need. Check out the SAP website for updates.

Question 06: Infotype

I am trying to create a bespoke infotype using transaction PM01 by keying in the new infotype number, and checking the "Module Pool" radio button. I go on putting in the infotype name and a couple of fields (e.g. endda begdda), save the details, and save it as object directory entry "Z001" (customer specified). When I activated it, I got the following error message:

"Table P9017 not active in ABAP Dictionary".

How can I fix it?

A: You can try the following procedures:

Procedure no: 1

Check if you have you used the transaction PM01. In here, you need to create the structure "PS9nnn", and then the modules and the screens. You can go for the 'create all' button.

After this, you need to maintain the infotype characteristics and the technical characteristics.

Under 'Infotype Characteristics', maintain the time constraints, single screen, (2000) and list screen (3000).

Doing all this will activate and prepare the basic framework for your infotype.

The further logic can be done in the 'Screen flow logic' of screen 2000.

Procedure No: 2

Here are the steps to create a new Infotype:

1. Go to transaction code PM01;
2. Type the new Infotype (starting with 9);
3. Create the PS structure;
a. Type in the desired fields;
b. Check -> Save -> Generate;

4. Create all;

5. Click IT Characteristics (or F5);

a. Select the new infotype;

b. Click details (or F2) in change mode;

c. Type in the required fields;

d. Save;

6. Click Technical Characteristics (or Shift+F);

a. Select the new infotype;

b. Click details (or F2) in change mode;

c. Type in the required fields;

d. Save;

Question 07: Blocking SSN

Is there any easy way to block the SSN (personnel ID number) on IT0002?

We do not want all the users to have access to this information, and we want to grant it on a need-to-know basis.

The security person at my company asked me what is the best approach would be, but I wasn't really sure.

I know I can use the feature P0002 via T588m to control this, but we want to create this authorization based on the user groups. The structure for P0002 does not carry UGR. We do not want to completely suppress the field for all the users.

Should I create a screen variant and use a user exit?

What is the best way to control this?

A: I don't think there's any such thing as field level authorization in SAP HR. The concept of info types is that they are groupings of related fields, so if you can see one you should be able to see all.

T588M and UGR are useful if it's only the view you're interested in, but this isn't security based.

The only solution I can think of is to copy I0002 to a customer info type, where you have complete control over the contents and can hide SSN. Remove I0002 from the relevant role, and then add the customer 0002 instead.

Question 08: Code of Conduct

Where can I find the "code of conduct", or related field to input
the code of conduct in SAP HR?

A: You can try using Infotype 41 (Date specifications), create
date type z1 as a code of business conduct, and input the date
when the employee signed.

Question 09: PA30

I used PA30 to create a new personnel number while I use
actions infotype to create an organizational assignment. But I
can't input position 9999, and 9999 does not appeared in the
drop box even if I already defined 9999 as position in IMG OG30
transaction (I maintained entry like object:S, position:9999).
When I create time sheet default infotype, the controlling area is
empty. By law it should be a default value. Thus, I can't save.

How can I resolve this?

A: You can use PA40 instead. It is intended for hiring. PA30 is
for maintenance of infotype. Regarding time sheet, you can use
PA61, list entry option.

Question 10: Display only option

In ESS, there is a standard scenario to enable employees to view and change their own employee data. I need to make this a 'Display only' option. To change any personal information entry, the employee needs to submit a document proof to HR Department e.g. Marriage Certificate, or passport.

It used to be possible in the ITS version, but I can't see any other way of doing it in the ESS Business Package Webdynpro stuff on EP. I'm working on mySAP ERP 2004 with EP 6.0 and ESS Business Package.

How can I execute this?

A: We had a similar issue where we found that users had access to change data for certain infotypes which we didn't want them to. We had to get an ABAPer to change the transaction for that infotype access to PA20 rather than PA30.

Question 11: Configuring Dynamic Actions

I am trying to configure Dynamic Actions for Infotype 8 (PY-INDIA). We are calling IT 8 after a User Defined IT via Dynamic Action, and it has been called successfully.

Can we pass Dynamic Variables to Dynamic action to default the values?

For example: WGTYP 3ADP needs to be assigned to any one in between BET01....BET19; How can this be done successfully?

A: You can do a set of plausibility checks (they show as "P") in your dynamic action, so you can tailor the dynamic action based on business rules.

Also check and look at feature LGMST and related configurations for defaulting in wage types into IT8. You can go with the feature over dynamic actions if it's a good fit.

Question 12: Changed data report

I got a request from our HR department to have a report that shows a changed data, and "changed by" for all employees belonging to a specific PA. That should be an 'output list' and would enable control if the proper procedures are followed. The report should show only changed data in a specific timeframe.

How can this be done?

A: You could use the Audit Report RPUAUD00.

Alternatively, you could write Ad Hoc or SAP Queries to give you the correct data on the various info types by outputting the "changed on" and "changed by" fields.

Question 13: Validity for infotype records

I hired someone on 08/01/2006. When hiring, I created a new 378 with the start date of 08/01/2006. When I get to the enrollment transaction, it is showing the "validity period" as 10/30/2006.

Where does the system calculate this date from?

In the 2 steps in the IMG, 1 "define admin parameters". I didn't do any changes, so the validity for infotype records is from the key date. In the step where I define the adjustment reason, the validity of infotype records is set to "adj. reason date". I thought this was correct. We are on ECC 5.0 with HR pack number 19 SAPKE50019.

Is there any other place to look for setting the validity for infotype records?

A: For the benefits, the 'adjustment reason date' is the selection period defaulted for the benefit program, not the 'date of entry'. If you want the 'date of entry', you need to flag 'date of offer' and tick anytime in the time frame.

Question 14: Notes on infotypes

SAP enables you to make notes on infotypes. You will get a "Word-like" text editor where you can make your notes. My question is, can I report on these notes?

This would be very useful if I can do that.

Is it possible to delete an already entered note?

A: Reading is possible with "Fm hr_read_infty_note".

The input parameter is the same key as in cluster table PCL1. This is where notes are stored.

Maybe manipulation of this data can be done with "FM hr_infotype_operations", or else check that function group HRMM for something useful.

Question 15: Enhancing infotype

I created an infotype, and I want it to behave in a way that if the data in a particular field already exists, it will show a warning message. Just like in IT Communication, if the number already exists in an existing employee, it shows a warning message to which the number already exists.

Where can I enhance infotype?

A: It sounds to me that this requirement needs a user exit. There are different types of user exits. You can do a quick search and you will get the information you need.

Another suggestion is if you are working on an infotype you created, you can insert code anywhere you want. Have a look at your code in your module pool.

Take note: MPXXXX00 where XXXX = your infotype.

Question 16: Create infotype 0041

I have created a dynamic action to create infotype 0041 in the background, but whenever PA41 is used to change a start date a duplicate record is created in infotype 0041.

Is there any place where can I look?

A: Try deleting IT0041 from the info group that is set up for your intended action. If you haven't done this yet, it might be worth giving a try.

SAP R/3 HR Tcodes

Payroll

Question 17: SAP HR Payroll India Module

I am using SAP HR Payroll India Module. I am trying to create a new action for an existing employee. This employee belongs to an employee subgroup TM, and has action type 'Hiring'. When I tried to create a new action type 'Leaving', I received an error message 'Assignment to feature IGMOD did not take place'. When I double clicked on this error message, it stated:

Assignment to feature IGMOD did not take place
Message no. P0603

Diagnosis:
You can assign a specific operation (assignment) to each decision option within a feature. You can also define decision option ** whose assignment is effected for all unlisted decision options (this is known as a default value).

Example:

D PERSK
K1 &ABRKS=D1, <- D1 for employee subgroup K1
K2 &ABRKS=D1, <- D1 for employee subgroup K2
K3 &ABRKS=D2, <- D2 for employee subgroup K3
** &ABRKS=D0, <- D0 for all other employee subgroups
If you now create employee subgroup K4 and the default entry ** is missing,
the system is unable to find a decision option for payroll area ABRKS.

Procedure:
Define a decision option for K4 or for default value **.

I don't know how to define a decision option. I am getting the same error message for all employees belonging to the employee subgroup TM.

Is there a way to correct this?

A: It seems that your feature IGMOD is missing some entries. You can use transaction PE03 to view the feature IGMOD, and read the tree to see what's wrong.

Question 18: Payroll deletion

Is it possible in QA / Pre-Prod client to delete all the payroll results from the last payroll for a certain payroll area?

A: If by "last payroll" you mean the last payroll period run in the history, then the answer is yes. However, it's 'onerous'.

You can select for each employee the period you wish to delete. There's no easy way to select just the last period for an employee. Depending on your payroll size, it could take a while although it wouldn't take long to write an ABAP to do it.

Question 19: Payroll configuration

How can I configure the payroll system?

What does it need to configure and run a payroll for an employee?

Are there any configuration documents?

A: The basic things which go into payroll processing are the following:

1. Payroll areas, period parameters and payroll calendar.
2. LGMST - feature returns allowance model and links all the allowable wage types to each allowance model. The automatic defaulting of wage types based on pay scale area, pay scale type, pay scale group and pay scale level in Infotype 8.
3. RAP - all allowance models to be linked with custom defined wage types created in the company.
4. Enterprise structure - personal areas, personal sub areas, employee groups, and employee sub group creation.
5. Wage type creations - Personal administration module.
6. Time Management - work schedule creation and linking of work schedule with employee in infotype 7.

The data in Infotype 0, 1, and 7 is mandatory. Allowances can be stored in Infotype 8, 14, 15, 57, etc.

Investments, Tax, Arrears, Benefits, Off-cycle payroll, cumulation, processing, and evaluation classes of wage types, priority of deductions, loans, posting configurations, etc. form part of payroll configurations as well.

You can also refer to SAP.help.com. It is excellent resource for learning the basics.

SAP provides pre-configured data for most of the nodes in Payroll. You can run the payroll without any configurations in the start. All the things above are pre-configured with standard values in SAP, but you need to customize your own payroll based on your requirements.

Question 20: SAP HR Terminologies

What does the following means: HCM, HRM, and HCM?

A: HCM is the new name of HRM in the never ending attempts of both SAP Marketing, as well as the same attempts of professors within the HR Area to ensure a positive cash flow.

HRM means Human Resources Management.

Meanwhile, HCM means Human Capital Management.

Question 21: Run payroll without BSI interface

Is it possible to run payroll without BSI interface?

Can we maintain any tables or any substitute which would help us in taxes (as the client has only 'Personal area' and very few employees)?

A: You can calculate gross and net in SAP and manage everything. You don't need BSI to do your taxes.

Question 22: Annual values in Payroll

We have 3 pay frequencies to cater for (weekly, fortnightly and monthly). The user want annual values only on IT0008, I'm not sure payroll can handle that. But even if it couldn't, it would save me a lot of hassle if I could store the annual values in T510 and convert them to period values on the IT0008 screen.

Is there any way I can record the annual values in the pay scale tables rather than duplicating my entries for each of my pay frequencies?

A: The pay frequency is the payroll area on IT0001 and should have no bearing on IT0008. You can set up your pay scales annually.

Set up whatever wage types you want. Nothing is wrong with an annual wage type. SAP Payroll can also be configured to look at ANSAL annual salary instead. In fact, if all you are entering is an annual salary on IT8, then it should be a breeze.

Question 23: Rule

I need to print a text (message) in the customized pay slip when a particular wage type exists in the payroll results. I tried to use 'Rule', but it didn't go through. I don't know what I did wrong when I was defining the 'rule'.

What can be the correct procedure for this?

A: It should be possible. You can use the following to do something similar:

Z1 01 RT LGART C EQ 1234 TEXT 01

Where 1234 is the wage type and 01 is the text field you have defined.

Question 24: Manual data entry

My company is upgrading FI/CO & MM to MYSAP 2005, and introduced BW.

We are also strongly considering the introduction of Payroll/HR as a completely new in house solution. The current payroll is outsourced.

We have had a high level demo from SAP which ticked almost every box. However, our payroll manager is still not convinced about the ease of entering manual daily timesheets for multiple employees (i.e. on/off times or absence reasons).

We have upwards of 5000 employees, with around half having data captured via a third party product (Kronos) which then feeds to the outsource agency system. The other 'half' was recorded via an employee group manual timesheets wherein a specific location manager sends in for 1 - 100 employees type scenario.

What can be the solution on manual data entry in the payroll screens for employee groups on a daily basis for the actual work?

A: You can consider having customized batch programs to upload the timesheet data submitted by the managers. This will add about half a day of activity for the payroll process.

Or you can consider having employees enter their own time on the portal using CATS and ESS. You can also put in approvals by managers, if required.

The last suggestion is to have an automatic flat file interfaces between KRONOS and SAP that is supported as a complementary software partner by SAP. But you should check on this.

Question 25: Q & A DB

How can I generate the Q & A database using ASAP tool?

Can I get a country specific questionnaire?

A: You need to add the project modules into scope and generate a report. This will prepare a word or an excel file depending on the type of report you generate.

For Payroll you can get country specific questionnaire. ASAP Q & A Db is used a lot specially during new implementations. It's SAP's recommended way if you want the implementation done quicker and more efficiently.

Question 26: Retention of employee numbers and payroll history

There are a bunch of employees that were transferred into a wrong organizational structure.

Is it possible to terminate them and re-hire them keeping the same employee numbers?

Is there anyway to keep their payroll history after they are terminated?

A: Just a suggestion, in case payroll has not run since and there are no such complications, you can just delete the last action and replace it with the right action. Try this on the test system first and ensure there is no dangerous impact.

Termination and Re-hire is a process supported by SAP, but it is too drastic for a remedy for your current problem. All that may be required is to find out a way to replace the incorrect organizational assignment information with the correct one.

Question 27: Table T52EL

How can I edit the table T52EL ?

A: The proper way would be to go into the IMG and do it there.

Under payroll--> Reporting for Posting Payroll Results to Accounting etc.

You can also go straight to the table V_T52EL_COMP.

Question 28: Cluster

What is a cluster?

How can I view an existing payroll result in SAP?

A: A cluster is a table. For performance and historical reasons, it is set up differently and this means it's difficult to view or download it like a standard table.

SAP have a range of SAP reports starting with "RPCLST**" to let you view the cluster you're interested in e.g. for UK payroll RPCLSTRG. There are many other alternative methods.

PU01 deletes payroll results, so don't use it to view clusters.

Question 29: Basic inquiries

Is there a good document which explains the configuration of payroll?

Also, are there any companies in the USA that are willing to hire a fresh graduate for some hands on configuration experience?

A: You can pick-up the HR400, Payroll configuration, and HR410 Payroll Configuration US.

Once you go through those training, you will be able to do a lot in Payroll.

The best way to get the experience is to work. You maybe able to get a chance to work for a company where they have implemented PY, but a company that will let you practice on their working system. It's a bit doubtful because no one would want to let a fresher practice on their production environment. After all, they are dealing with thousands of employees' paycheck.

Question 30: Leave without pay

I am implementing an India specific payroll for the first time.

How can I organize 'Leave without Pay' in the customizing?

A: To summarize the steps:

* store the results in 'Time clusters';
* 'hand over' the monthly cumulative to payroll;
* multiply number of hours by hourly wage;
* add this amount as a negative amount to GTN;

Question 31: Inter-company postings

Is Payroll able to post inter-company postings?

For example, Company A pays for Company B's employee salaries. We want to generate an entry where the payroll expense/ payable go against the paying company, in this case, Company A.

If this is possible, what changes do we need to make to Payroll Configuration?

A: As far as payroll postings is concerned, if you have assigned a cost center to a person in an organizational assignment and if that cost center belongs to a different controlling area, then the System doesn't allow this posting.

E.g. if a person belongs to X company code and his cost center in organizational assignment belongs to Y company code, you will find a problem in postings with error message. To handle this, you can try some user exits.

But if you want to do cross company postings, you have to assign the cost centers in cost distribution info type. In this case, there will be no error messages.

Actually, this can be also done for liabilities. For example, you want to post Net Pay to a corporate company code from all others, you set the symbolic account type to "FL" and create a technical account for inter-company posting with account key "1001" and insert your inter-company G/L number. Then, you have to change your user exit in RPCIPE00 to change the internal table ep-bukrs for the symbolic account to the corporate company code (whatever that may be), also referred to as "paying company code" This has only been added in early 2004.

Question 32: Down system while in the middle of payroll activities

Our PRD system went down today and we don't have a back up. Worst, we were in the middle of our payroll activities. We had exited payroll and were running our FICO postings. We are still not sure why the system is down and the basis team has been working on it. We were to send our direct deposit files and print checks by tomorrow and get the payroll done with. The direct deposit file was supposed to go out by today.

Is there anyway we can print a check for all the EEs and suspend the direct deposits once we get our system back and running?

Or is it possible to print checks out of QAS or sandbox anyway for all the EEs after we get the 'up to date' master data into QAS or sandbox?

We are in a fix right now and can't move any further till our basis team gets back to us with answers.

Is there anything at all we can do other than just sitting and waiting for a response?

A: I have been faced with something like this once before. We found it was easiest to resend the previous period bank file, and then when the system comes up, do a net pay comparison and adjust people as required. This will of course miss any starters and leavers for this period, but in a situation like this I would rather pay 90% of people about right than 100% not at all.

I don't know of a way that you could do change all your employees to check payments. I suppose you could restore a copy of prod back onto a QA box, get an ABAPER to write an update program to change everyone to payment method check, then run payroll and your check program over them.

Another option could be to create a custom copy of your check generation program and change the information that it reads so it picks up all employees with payments, rather than those who are identified as checks.

Question 33: Changing payroll

We are trying to change the payroll area of weekly employees to bi-weekly in a plant.

How can I do that for the inactive (terminated) employees since they might get some bonus by the end of the year?

A: You can try the following method:

You need to re-instate the employee as if you are trying to pay a bonus. After that, change their payroll area by way of an action. And then terminate after the payment is done.

SAP R/3 HR Tcodes

Salary

Question 34: ABKRS feature

I need a structure like the following:

Personnel Area (Ex: New York)

Personnel Sub area (Ex: Sales)

Return value (Ex: Monthly)

Employee Subgroup (Ex: Engineer)

Return Value (hourly)

In the above structure, employees belonging to New York and sales department will get monthly salary. On the other hand, employees belonging to New York and occupying the role of Engineer will be getting hourly wages.

Can we structure such a scenario?

A: You can try the following code:

```
0010 D MOLGA
0020 10 D WERKS
0030 10 NY D PERSK
0040 10 NY Engineer &ABKRS="hourly"
0050 10 NY * &ABKRS = "monthly"
0060 10 * &ABKRS ="99"
0070 * * &ABKRS = "99"
```

Question 35: Automatic salary increase

We are planning to award 1% automatic salary increase to our 10,000 employees next month through our enterprise company management sub module.

Is there any single transaction where we can award this salary increase, or do we need to develop a program to get this done?

A: For a payment increase, you can setup a record in table T510 for the specific grade and the wage type using variant 'D'. You can also add the percentage as well.

When running report RPITRF00, you have to make sure the date of the collective agreement is the same as the one specified in table T510D. Then, a new record in IT0008 will be created from that date with the payment increase.

Question 36: Appearance of wage type

When I run the Sims for a particular employee for the month of September, /ZMN is appearing. This was not seen when payroll was run for August. But now when I run Sims for the previous months, /ZMN is seen in the pay slips of August.

There were changes to IT7; IT8 on 31.08.2006.IT7 was again changed on 06.09.2006 for the previous months. The employee was on SMP which ended on 06.05.2006.

Why is the wage type appearing?

A: The /Z wage types are due to retro changes. You should find a /A* wage type in the retro period results being saved into the DT, and then current period run creating the /ZMN from it.

Track this /A* wage type through your retro log and you'll find why it's being created.

Question 37: New wage types

I am using SAP HR Payroll India. I have created two new wage types.
I am using these two wage types as 'Additional Payments'. I want to add these two wage types in the gross total. But I don't want to add the amount of these two wage types for calculating the basis of 'Professional Tax' and ESIC.

How can I exclude these two wage types from the ptax, basis, and ESIC basis?

What configuration steps should I follow?

A: Wage type processing/cumulating classes and evaluation bases are stored and can be displayed from table "V_512W_O" or "V_512W_D".

Go to transaction SM31. Select the table, click on 'display change', enter 'country grouping', select 'wage type' and click on 'Details' icon.

The system will display the attributes of a wage type for payroll processing.

Before changing one of the attributes, you need to be sure about the retroactive accounting impacts, etc.

Question 38: Overtime calculation

I have created a wT under 2010, and my OT calculation is as follows:

If the number of hours worked is > 8 hrs, then OT should be twice the hourly rate of Basic pay.

I even tried creating a PCR, but it failed.

I modified PCR X935, tried to set a custom wage type, and calculate by Amt/26/8.

BWGRL Valuation basis per hour

STDAZ Number of hours

ABRTP Payroll days in payroll period

RTE=0 /9001 The WT is read from VORT

RTE= 9001 * to access 9001 WT at the time of processing the schema.

The collected above information is for the creation of my PCR, but was halted half-way.

How should I proceed?

A: You can try something along this lines which should have most of the variables you need:

Z001 Personnel Calculation Rule Z001
--> *
-->9000 Misc. Deduction
--> AMT?8 Comparison
--> >
NUM=2.0 Set
MULTI NRA Multipl.amt/no/rate
ADDWT * OT Output table
--> *
ADDWT * OT Output table

Question 39: Copying standard wage type

I am configuring Lebanon country setup for an existing system. While I am trying to copy the standard wage types, I did not find the standard wage types in the create wage type catalog.

Is it necessary to apply OSS note to update T512W table for LB?

A: There is a chance that there are no WTs for Lebanon as a standard. You can probably find this out by looking in client 000. This client contains all the sap standard table entries.

If there are in fact no valid entries for Lebanon (as is the case for many countries), then probably the best way to create them is to copy them from another country. You can do this by creating a custom version of PU30 (with some help from an ABAPER) that allows you to copy WTs from one country code to another.

Question 40: Additional allowance

When an employee completes 20 years from the date of confirmation, he needs to be paid an additional allowance like the Senior Service Pay.

Are there some ways of automatically triggering this?

A: The easiest way is to run a report on everyone's length of service and input the data manually. Otherwise, you could go for a payroll rule that automatically generates a payment based on the length of service.

Question 41: Wage type and benefits

We need to hire an employee for the first three months on probationary period. In that period, he is eligible for the basic pay, HRA, DA. After finishing his probationary period, he is eligible to avail other benefits like mobile expenses, car, relocation expenses, and etc.

Is there any possible way to add other wage type to that particular employee after 3 months of the hiring date?

A: Yes, there is. You can just create an IT 15 / IT14 record for these wage types with a start date 3 months after the person's hire date. There's no additional configuration required as long as you have the wage types already set up.

Question 42: Balance sheet account

When I do the FI posting for the fourth period (Aug), I get no error. But when I run for the third period (Test mode), I get an error and /559 is missing under the balance sheet account.

How do I get /559 under the balance sheet account?

A: You just need to make sure you've got this wage type linked to an appropriate balance sheet symbolic account.

Check T52EL to see if you've linked this to an account such as 'salaries'.

The most important thing is that the account type is an 'F'.

Question 43: Pre-noted direct deposit accounts

For US employees, we don't always want new Direct Deposit accounts to be pre-noted.

Is there a way to flag or override the bank accounts so that they don't go through the pre-notification process?

A: We had been creating pre-notes for quite some time. Our reject rate was so low the customer made a business decision to stop the pre-note process.

The customer stopped executing RPCDTEU0 and RFPNFC00. The employees now have their first payments going to the respective bank as directed by the employee.

Question 44: Retro active accounting

I have used clusters to pick payroll data. Everything is working fine except retro active accounting. It is being correctly done by RPCEDTK0. I could find one Function Module 'HR99L00_GET_ACTUAL_AND_ORIG_RT' but I don't know how to use it.

Which Wage Type should be used for that?

A: If I have understood your problem correctly, you want to post payments relating to previous periods.

You can try using wage types /551 and /552. They are used for retro accounting.

Question 45: Remuneration Statement

We have some employees who are paid by the entry of a set of wage types in IT0015. The P0015-BEGDA is the date the payment is being made for, and a Number of Units is also specified to determine the amount payable.

The current format of our standard Remuneration Statement only has room to display the Wage type Text, Number, and Amount (for payment Wage types).

We have been asked to provide a version of the Remuneration Statement for this group of employees that will display Wage type Text, Date (P0015-BEGDA), Number, and Amount.

Is there a way to read the P0015-BEGDA details when generating the Remuneration Statement?

A: The best way would be to use structure V0, and move the BEGDA of the infotype record to structure V0 when you are reading the infotype data within the payroll schema.

You can use operation XV0 to generate the relevant entries.

SAP note 654119 gives more information on this query.

SAP R/3 HR Tcodes

Schedule

Question 46: Time evaluation

Our company just used 'time clock' data to do evaluation, no in and out times. I ran ZTIME to upload the data. It does update the time sheet of the specified EE. I ran CAT2 and I can see all the attending hours corresponding to relative attendance type. But when I ran 'time evaluation', no data was read from the time sheet. It says the EE was not at work. I am sure the period for the time data and evaluation is right.

What could be the problem?

A: ZTime looks like some custom report. First of all, check in PA61 and see if the Time data really came in properly and populated the infotypes.

Then, look in IT0007. Confirm if you the following procedure was done.

CAT2 records the time. Then, you have to use CATA for transferring all the modules and CAT6 to transfer to HR. Once this is done, you should see all the 'Time data' in the infotypes.

Question 47: Hire date

Our SAP started in '98 and all the cost centers were created valid from that year. Now, we want to implement HR but the problem we are facing is the system is not allowing the employee hire date earlier to the 'cost centre create date'.

Obviously, we have employees hired before SAP started and we are facing a problem in keying in their actual hire date. Alternatively, we created another field called 'technical date of entry' and we are using it to enter the hire date.

Is there anyway that we can have the actual hire date as the 'begin date' for the employee for all those employees who were there before the cost center (controlling area) started functioning?

A: You are migrating through LSMW or directly you are creating in SAP. You can try to switch off the integration between PA and OM after creating the employee record switch on the integration.

If you don't switch on integration it defaults position 9999999. Later, you can change it to the correct position and assign cost center as well.

Another suggestion is to create all master data records starting with a conversion hire date and record the Original Hire Date on IT0041. This way, you don't need to be concerned about objects and have the ability to report on all the relevant dates.

Question 48: Off cycle

When I run off cycle, it displays "Day of Bonus payment to be specified".

How can I do this?

A: For off cycle payroll run:

1. Bonus or which off cycle pay component record to be there in infotype 267, the off cycle payments with the date of payment e.g. 5th Sept. 2006.

2. When running off cycle run, enter the date 5th Sept. 2006 in the date field specified.

Question 49: Working time

My client has around 20 shifts operational in a month. The duty roster i.e. planned working time is planned weekly. The planned working time could however change at any point in time.

Time recording system is in place to punch the 'time in' and 'time out' of the employee. However, the most important thing is there is no salary deduction for less hours work or no extra overtime pay for extra hours worked. Only if there are no 'time in' and no 'time out' for a single day for an employee who will mark the employee as absent.

The solution we are proposing is presented below:

1. Create as many daily work schedules, period work schedules, and monthly work schedules as there are shifts in the company. Maintain them in Infotype 7 and keep on modifying whenever there is change in planned working time of an employee.

2. Use Attendance infotype 2002 to store the actual hours worked everyday. If there are no 'time in' and 'time out' data, the batch upload program will create a 'loss of pay' absence record in the absence infotype.

3. Various reports for less hours worked, extra hours worked, planned hours, actual hours worked, etc. will be fetched through sap query or custom developed solutions.

Since there is no link of actual hours worked with Payroll, we are not going for 'Time evaluation' module.

Is the above solution good enough, or should 'Time evaluation' will be the best way to go for it?

A: In situation like this, I would suggest going for 'time evaluation'. You can have a great control and flexibility regarding to shifts. When you go for positive time evaluation, it is easy to capture 'clock in' and 'clock out' times. If there are no 'clock in' and 'clock out' times, we can consider them as there are no planned working hours. Your approach is quite good towards solution.

Question 50: Shifting of schedules

We are implementing 'Time management' for a hotel industry here. The industry has several shifts in which the employees come in for work. There is a system which records the clock-in and out timings.

The scenario is that the shift timing of an employee could change any day within a particular month. Hence, their duty roster keeps on changing.

Shift timings are normally for 8 hours and the earliest shift could start around 6 in the morning, and the last shift could end around 8 the next morning.

How should I go about configuring this?

A: These are just possibilities. You could use a substitution like swapping daily work schedule infotype 2003. It depends on the frequency if this is too much of a manual adjustment.

You could create a flexible daily/period work schedule.

You could look at dynamic daily work schedules and see if a rule can be applied that would match your clock time.

Question 51: Accrual in time

I am looking for a solution for an issue with accrual in time. I know basic configuration in time management, but I'm not good in PCR's and schemas.

Due to requirement change, I need to change PCR which is calculating accrual based on date from it0045.

Currently, it is calculating based on service date from 41 according to the employee's individual service anniversary.

PCR:
D HRS=YDAY01HRS?1
HRS=10.00 ADDDBQ090
HRS=10.00 ADDDBQ090
D HRS?2
HRS=12.00 ADDDBQ090
HRS=12.00 ADDDBQ090....Etc

The new requirement is it should increase on the first day of January on the calendar year. Like if the employee joined on Dec. 2006, he should get accrual on Jan2007, so there is no difference. If he joins in Jan. or Dec. he will get accrual on next January. We are using schema copy of TM04. Time evaluation id is running daily.

How can I achieve this?

A: You should look to return your system to standard absence quota generation.

The problem you will find is that you're using time evaluation to generate a full year entitlement, but time evaluation will only work correctly with accruals.

There was a previously implemented holiday system which has the flexibility of accruals, but a full-year entitlement, using standard absence quota configuration, dynamic actions, and user exits. So it can be done, but it does take a while.

Question 52: Overtime record

If the work schedule of an employee is from 8:30 to 17:30, the time event for clock out is 20:00. After time evaluation, the time from 17:30 to 20:00 automatically creates an overtime record.

We want to add one more approval step. The supervisor approves the overtime record. If the over time record is not approved, the time from 17:30 to 20:00 will not be taken as overtime.

How can I do this?

A: Your best option is to use attendance quota. The overtime will then only be processed by Time Evaluation if the relevant quota has been created.

Question 53: Absence quota

I couldn't create an absence quota for this scenario because the amount of days is not fixed.

For example, if an employee works a complete month he can accrue 2.5 days leave. He can use that leave within that year, so per year it should be 30 days. But I have to create this quota if the employee works.

How do we implement this?

A: The way I understand it, if an employee works for a full month without taking any leave, he gets 2.5 days for that month, otherwise he gets zero. These are for permanent full time employees. So, if time evaluation is not there, we can think of a custom program similar to "rptqta00" which will be run at the end of every month. It will upload 2.5 days to IT 2006, if employee has full attendance within the month.

If, on the other hand, it is a question of prorating 30 days per year according to days worked, then "rptqta00" should be able handle it as standard.

Question 54: Leave quotas

We want to implement a new leave quota which is 6 days full paid sick leave per anniversary year.

Is it possible to fill up all quotas upon each start of the anniversary year?

How can we do this with the standard implementation?

A: It is possible to fill the quota automatically, there are two ways.

First is on the manual way. Run a report "PRPTQTA00", and it will generate the quotas as specified in the Quota Generation Rules.

The second way is through the schema "TQTA". Incorporate this schema in your payroll schema and configure the rules.

Question 55: Public holidays

When an employee switched from a defined 'Public holiday' for cover e.g. Bank Holiday is Monday, but they take preceding Friday as Bank Holiday and are planning to work Monday. But on the Monday, the employee goes off sick.

We have already booked the preceding Friday as Bank holiday. The planned hours for Monday showed as nil (as according to Work Schedule, this is the expected day off). We can't book any absence hours on this day as the system reduces them to a max of planned hours from WS (in this case nil).

I checked the configuration for absences, and changed from 'Error' to 'warning'. I also made sure the day calendar is set to "K" Calendar Days.

According to the WS the Holiday Class is 1 (Pub Holiday), and the Day Type is 1 (Day Off). We are using Version 4.7 and booking times via CATS (CAT2). We do not use Time Evaluation or SAP Payroll.

Is it possible to book absences on these day types that has zero planned hours, and if so which settings do I need to change/look at?

A: Try using 'Substitution', and put in the nil hours as a working day. Then book an absence against it.

Question 56: Backdate an initial hire date

Is there anyway to backdate an initial hire date if payroll has already been run?

I need to backdate an EE to about a month before the hire date that is on the system right now, and the payroll for this period has already been processed and exited.

I know a work around is just do the correction on the payroll side using a one time payment to settle the difference.

Is there anyway we can fix the record?

A: Try this process in sandbox before proceeding to the production server.

First, you have to remove the present date from Infotype, 02 Payroll Status (Earl.pers. RA dat) and (Accounted to) and then try to change the entry date to backdate.

After changing the backdate, reset the date in payroll status.

Question 57: Termination date

I have a problem with termination date whenever I terminate an employee. E.g. I terminated an employee on 07/01/2006, the date automatically changes to the past or future but not specific to the date I have given.

What are the configuration changes I have to do?

A: This can be controlled on T529A. You can do it with the date control field AUSDT. You need to define by each of your action types what date to default. For example, if the term date is also the last date worked, then leave this field blank. If the term date is the day after the last date worked, enter a "1" in the date control field and the system will add 1 day to the date of execution.

Question 58: Service joining date

This is WRT, a public sector company in India. The client where we are implementing SAP is recruiting Ex-Army/Ex-Navy employees.

For calculating the service, we are storing service joining date in 'date specification'. But if an employee has worked for 10 years in the army, and then there will be break in service for 5 years and if he joins the organization, we have to consider only ten years of his earlier service.

How do we maintain the service joining date in date specification?

A: You can treat it the same way for someone who has been separated from the company and been rehired. You need to use different dates in 0041 though.

Question 59: Overlapping schedule

Our client has this 9X80 work schedule rule. Where in the 'Work Week' starts on a Friday and ends on the Friday. An employee is allowed to work 9 hours for the first 4 days, and 8 hours on Friday. The 4 hours of the Friday are a portion to the next week's Friday, and they can take off on the next Friday.

So we have 2 issues here. One is for time management, we have to take the 4 hours of the Friday and put them on the next week.

For Payroll, the pay period is starting on Friday PM and ending on Friday AM.
E.g. Start day of the pay period is 01/06/2006 (Friday) and End date is 01/20/2006 (Friday). Now, the next pay period is starting on 01/20/2006 and ending on 02/03/2006. So, the End date of the first pay period is the same as the start date of the 2nd Pay period.

I know that system allows you to have the overlapping start and end dates, but when I am running the payroll it is taking the previous and next payroll periods also (overlapping periods).

Is there any different setting that I need to make in order for system to pick only the current pay period?

A: As for the first part, you could use a time type and have hours on one Friday got added on a time type. Then, a PCR in time evaluation to "pay" the hours on the following Friday if the employee doesn't work and they have hours in the time type.

We have a 9 day fortnightly roster that, if their 10th roster day off falls on a public holiday, the day off rolls forward to the next working day. We use 2 PCR's in time evaluation and a time type to track the owed hours.

SAP R/3 HR Tcodes

Benefits

Question 60: Configuring benefit eligibility

How can I configure benefit eligibility based on zip code and salary?

How can I accomplish this?

A: You can try to place it where you want to input the benefits information while doing 'new starter' process. If you want to input benefits in 'new starter' or any action process, create a dynamic action based on salary and post code.

You may also need to create both a zip code group and a salary group for your plans, and assign these groups to each of the plans.

Question 61: Configuring a medical opt out

How do we configure a medical opt out in R/3 and ESS?

Those who opt out get $50 per month.

A: You need to create it as a medical plan and have the amount of $50.00 coded as a credit to the employee if you are also running payroll.

Question 62: Configure by rules of schema

On a public holiday, the salaried employees are paid whether they show up for work or not. If the employee works on a public holiday, they are to be paid as follows:

ATTN CODE Description

ATN1 8 hrs of public holiday + 8 hrs of 2X Time = 36 hours pay (ALREADY WORKING FINE)
ATN2 8 hrs of 2X time = 24 hours pay (NEED TO CREATE)

How can this be taken care of?

Example:
26 Dec ATN1 --> 8 hrs of public holiday + 8 hrs of 2X Time = 36 hours pay
27 Dec ATN2 --> 8 hrs of 2X time = 24 hours pay

How can this be configured by the rules in the schema, so that appropriate wage types are generated?

In our T510S, we got the rules required to generate the appropriate wage types and its working fine for the WT for ATN1, but for ATN2 I am getting stuck.

My main problem is that in the TIP, there are some entries that are created by P2002 and so they fall under time pair origin indicator pair type P, D, E.

The record with Time pair origin indicator as 'P' is set to processing class 'M'.
The record with Time pair origin indicator as 'D' is set to processing class 'S'.

I need to process the S for one attendance code and not process it for another attendance code.

How can this be achieved?

A: You can try to add a calculation rule depending on the attendance type altered and the processing class to suit the desired further processing in Time Management.

This probably needs some alterations, but hopefully it will provide you with a good start.

OUTTPORIGS Origin status
*
COLOP* TIP >TOP curr.TType
R
FILLPVR Processing type
COLOP* TIP >TOP curr.TType

Question 63: Retention bonus

I have wired situation like the SAP-Payroll is not implemented in the Organization, but they have an external toll called as EDP. But the client has an employment retention program every year. It's like he hires an employee and promises him that if he stays in an organization for four years, he will be paid $20,000 for four years i.e. to be specific $5,000 every year. Hence, when the employee is hired, the employer plans it and gives him a 'Retention Bonus'. So, it's like he needs to enter it for e.g. in infotype 0015 for all the four years and whenever the particular year end comes, the client will pay him.

It's basically the future amounts of the Retention Bonus that has to be entered here, and when the time comes they transfer it to their 'External Toll'.

How can I execute this?

A: I think it is best put them onto infotype 15 as one 'off payments'. You can date these into the future, so when you hire them you could create a dynamic action to create four separate payments. You can check if you can get a dynamic action to add a year onto a date.

Question 64: ESS

I am able to see various functionality like Benefits, Payments, Working time, personal data change etc. when I sign in as an ESS User.

Would an employee receive messages in his normal company mailbox [e.g. outlook, lotus notes, etc]? Or would he also have a separate mailbox on the ESS homepage too?

Is there a facility for the same? And if yes, do I need to do some more configurations for the same?

A: An ESS user according to authorizations can use SAP Inbox functionality (SO01).

In order to receive SAP message in Outlook or Lotus notes inbox, you need to install SAP connect etc. You can check with your basis person.

With regards to 'Notification' on personnel data change, check feature M0001 - Parameter settings for mail on change to infotype record, and whether appropriate dynamic action is created.

Question 65: Vacation entitlement

Right now, I'm using SAP US version 4.7. We are using time evaluation for the quota only (TMS=7), schema TQTA.

We want vacation entitlement to be given to employees based on their hire date, and the quota is generated all at once.

0 -3 years 80 hrs
4-5 years 100 hrs
etc.

We need to run a report or something like that. It has to check the hire date of an employee, and if the hire date is in the month the program is run it has to generate the quota based on the above rules. The old quota has to be delimited or moved to other quota so that it can be used in this month only, and the new quota is valid for one year. If the hire date doesn't fall in the same month the program is run, it should not create quota. This program is run on the 20th of every month.

I was thinking if I can solve it by writing some rule to put in the schema. So, I can check the month of the employment from the dates infotype and check the current month.

How can I do that if it's possible?

A: If you're running time evaluation everyday, then this can be set up.

Here is a quick overview:

In your time schema you need to call function quota, this performs the leave accruals for quotas.

On your employee master data, check if you have IT41 date type setup. In there, you can store your original start date.

Assuming you also have IT2006 created for employees.

In SPRO/IMG in time management (Look at table T559L), you can set up your base entitlement based on seniority, so the number of hours granted 80 or 100 can be setup there. This is where you also set up the quota to be a daily or monthly accrual or up front grant.

Question 66: Health benefits

I have a situation where in we have to load a few EEs into our SAP system, but we don't process their payroll but only provide them with health benefits. The only reason they have to be on our system is because we need to keep track of the health costs for these set of people.

So, I created a new PY area and an action to load in all the necessary master data that needs to go to the third party benefit provider. I also created a new personnel sub area where I thought I can throw in all these people for whom we don't process the payroll.

Is there any other way I can approach this?

My main concern after doing all this is reporting as most of the reports is based on the employment status, and I wouldn't want our reports to pick these EEs when the users are running their reports for active EEs. I know we can use options to exclude EEs from reports based on the PY area or PSA, but that would mean recreating variants for users for all the reports.

Is there a better work around for this?

A: We are looking at putting non payroll processing employees on also. We will use a non payroll processing payroll area. The other thing we have set up is an "external" employee group.

Like you, I can see no other way than altering variants for existing reports. As it is, we use employee group in our selection criteria a lot, so the number of variants we have to change is few.

We couldn't see any other way around it, unless you use authorizations to prohibit users from reporting on an employee group or payroll area (depending on your version of SAP).

SAP R/3 HR Tcodes

Configuration Issues

Question 67: Configuration steps in MSS

We want to change the evaluation path for MSS so that managers who are not chiefs can see the people reporting to them. We have the position-to-position relationship set up in the organization, and can use the evaluation path S-S-P to display the correct people. But we are unclear as to the configuration steps necessary to make this happen in MSS.

What are the steps that need to be taken in the V_twpc* tables to change this?

A: You can try the following:

table v_twpc_v_c

Create a view ID and enter either an 'evaluation path' or a 'custom function' module in the following fields:

Evaluation Path for Root Object;
Function Module Root Object;
Evaluation Path Objects;
Function Module Object S;

You might need a custom function module for the root objects and a standard evaluation path, say B002 for the evaluation path objects.

You can try to explore further customizing options in IMG, Integration with Other mySAP.com Components, Business Packages/Functional Packages, Managers Self Service (my ERP 2004), and Object and Data provider in case you need to configure columns, columns headers, etc.

Question 68: Defaulting problem

In our system, when we create IT0021-subtype spouse, automatically the last name is defaulted with the employee's last name. The users do not want the defaulting function.

Where is it configured? How do we do away with it?

A: As far as I know, this is hard coded by SAP. Look at coding MP002100 and search for FANAM. You will see that FANAM is checked several times on blanks and filled by P0002-NACHN.

Maybe you can fill it yourself via a user-exit.

Question 69: Configuring the MSS

We are trying to configure the MSS for editing appraisals. The problem is that even after customizing the R/3 in the MSS, we don't see the appraisal form but instead we received an error message.

What should we do to correct this?

A: Try to check the following:

Check if the configuration has been carried out at IMG Path --> Personnel Management --> Personnel Development --> Objective Setting and Appraisals --> Edit Templates (Transaction PHAP_CATALOG_PA).

Check if the configuration is correct and the template has released status.

Check if all the workflow related settings are correct.

If you are using a portal make sure that the deployment is properly done.

Check the user Role or Authorization.

Check if the Homepage Framework configuration is correct.

Just take note that the above are pointers for diagnosis and not a solution.

Question 70: Final Confirm field

I would like to be able to enter the 'Final Confirm' field when using CAT2 to enter time data for PM Work Orders. I configured the 'Field Selection' and indicated that it is an input field. I have also deleted all previous influences by data entry profile. The final confirm field still remains hidden. I have tried doing this with the other fields and I am able to successfully change them from 'hidden' to 'input'.

How can I allow the input of the 'Final confirm' field and other related fields such as Partial confirm, remaining?

A: Double click in the 'hours' field. It should be in the pop-up rather than in the "main" CATS screen.

Question 71: Approving CATS timesheets

We are approving CATS timesheets through the transaction CAPP.

When an approver rejects time, we do not want the rejections to be sent anywhere. We would like the flag "send notification of rejection" not be defaulted with a tick.

How can I remove the defaulted flag within configuration, so that no approvers has this flag automatically set when they go into transaction CAPP?

A: You could either save a variant of CAPP without this box checked, or get the assistance of an ABAP guru to alter the code: 'mail like rcatstxx-rejection_mail default 'X' modif id bo1,' within the 'CATSSELE'. Include it so that the default is blank (unselected) rather than 'X', perhaps by using a custom include or a user exit.

SAP R/3 Transaction Codes for FICO

FICO Tcodes

General Questions and Answers

Question 01: CO Enterprise Structure

What is the enterprise structure of CO?

A: The controlling enterprise structure is nothing but maintaining controlling area and operating concern. The following are some materials regarding controlling enterprise structure.

The two sections that define the controlling enterprise structure are the controlling area and the operating concern. The controlling area is the central organizational unit within controlling module. A single company code can be assigned to only one controlling area. Establishing the controlling area is the first step in completing controlling configuration.

I. CONTROLLING AREA MAINTENANCE (OKKP/OX06)

Maintain controlling area
Activate components / control indicators
Assign company codes to controlling area
Assign number ranges to controlling area

A. Maintain controlling area:

Controlling area: Enter four digit alphanumeric identifier of your controlling area. If your controlling area will contain just one company code, select CO Area=CCode button. When prompted, enter the company code ID.

Name: Enter a description of your controlling area.

Distributions method: This field is relevant only of you area using SAP's Application Link Enabling (ALE) to link multiple R/3 systems together. If you are not using ALE, leave this field blank.

Logical system: This is relevant only if ALE is utilized. Enter the name of the central system for the controlling area.

CoCdàCo Area: This field is used to define the relationship between the company's code and the controlling area. You will have identified this relationship when you determined the controlling area ID. The options for this field are as follows:

(Controlling area same as company code): Use this if you have a one-to-one relationship between company code and controlling area.

(cross-company cost accounting): Use this if your controlling area will have two or more company codes assigned to it. This setting will activate cross-company cost accounting within the controlling area.

Currency type: This setting defines the type of currency used throughout the controlling area. Currency settings can be confusing. If you selected 1 in the CoCdàCO Area field, R/3 uses the default setting of 10, company code currency. If you selected 2, or cross-company cost accounting your choices expand. Use the pull down menu and the following options will appear.

- 10 (company code currency) Use this only if all the company codes assigned use the same currency.

- 20 (any currency) this selection offers the greatest amount of flexibility when choosing a controlling area currency. All other selections impose artificial constraints.

- 30(Group currency) this currency is maintained at the client level. Use this option to reconcile FI and CO ledgers.

- 40(hard currency) this can be used if the assigned company codes are from the same country and use the same Index-Based or group currency. This option is often used in countries where inflation is very high.
- (index based currency) this often used in countries where inflation is high or unstable. The currency is fabricated and in use to support external (outside the company) or used the same currency.

Currency: the entry made for currency type may influence your selection of a currency. Remember that you are defining the default currency for the controlling area only.

Chart of accounts (COA): Each controlling area can utilize only one chart of accounts. If you selected 1 in the CoCdàCO Area field, the system populates this field automatically with the company chart. If not, you must manually enter the chart name. Remember that all company codes assigned to the controlling area must use the same chart the controlling area uses.

Fiscal year variant: The variant must be the same for the assigned company codes and the controlling area.

B. Activate component / control indicators (OKKP):

Fiscal year: Enter the fiscal year when the activation settings become valid.

Cost centers: If you leave the box empty, cost center accounting is not activated. The possible entries from the drop-down list are as follows:

CCA is fully activated.
CCA is not activated, but you can use cost centers as account assignment objects. The cost center is validated /checked against the master data table. CO is not updated .utilize this setting if you do not want CCA active today but may want to activate it with the same cost center master data at some point in the future. You can then subsequently post all the cost center data to the CO files. Cost center must be created in full. CCA is not activated, but you can use cost centers as account assignment objects. The main difference is that cost centers do not have to be completed in full.

Order management: If you leave this empty, internal order accounting is inactive. Here are the other options for this field. Internal order accounting is fully activated.
Internal order accounting is not activated, but you can use order as account assignment objects. The order is then validated/ checked against the master data, including whether order has been released for postings. CO is not updated. Utilize this setting if you do not want internal orders active today but may want to activate them at some point in the future. You can then subsequently post all the internal orders data to the CO files.

Internal order accounting is not activated, but you can use internal orders as account assignment objects. The system doesn't check internal orders to see whether postings can occur: it only checks to see if they exist.

Commitment management: Use this field to determine whether commitments (for example, purchase requisitions and purchase orders) are updated for the controlling area. Leave this empty if you do not want to activate this function. Select 1 if you want commitment management activated.

Profit analysis: Use this field to define whether and how profitability analysis (CO-PA) is activated. SAP provides two types of CO-PA.Account-based and costing –based of the two, costing –based is more flexible and therefore more popular. Originally, only costing –based CO-PA existed. However, many accountants thought it was important to easily tie to the G/L, so SAP developed account-based CO-PA. Leave this field blank if CO-PA should not be activated. The options from the drop-down list are as follows:
-    Only costing –based CO-PA is activated.
-    Only account-based CO-PA is activated.
-    Both account and costing –based CO-PA is activated.

Activity based costing (ABC):
ABC is activated with restrictions. Allocations are posted as statistical entries on the cost object. The real posting would go to another CO object like a cost center. ABC is activated without restrictions.

Profit center accounting (PCA): Select this field if you want PCA to be activated.

Projects: if this field is not activated, project data within CO is not updated. WBS (Work Break –down Structure).
Sales orders: If you are utilizing make –to –order production, this setting becomes important. If you are not, leave this blank. If it's activated, all revenues and costs will post to the sales order items.

Cost objects: If you are using repetitive manufacturing within your product cost environment, this setting becomes relevant. Repetitive manufacturing uses cost objects to plan and track production costs.

All currencies: This setting will often default from your controlling area definition. If it's activated, the system will update CO values in the transaction currency and the object currency. If it's inactive, only the controlling area currency is used to update CO values.

Variances: Active this if you want SAP to calculate and post as a line item variances from each primary cost posting. Variances occur when the actual costs are less than or greater than planned costs. Actual and planned cost variances result when the actual price of the resources is less than or greater than the planned price.

Company code validations: These settings will automatically activate if cross-company code cost accounting is activated in the controlling area definition. If active, the setting will ensure that both sides of an accounting or purchasing transactions generate from a cost center in the same company code. Using the same criteria, it ensures that all inventory activities are posted properly in both company codes.

When you're done configuring the control indicators then save your settings. You will notice that SAP has filled 9999 in the valid to field of the fiscal year range. The settings are valid until year 9999 or until you make an entry for a new fiscal year.

C. Assign Company codes to controlling area (OKKP):

Either place your cursor on the controlling area you want to maintain or select the button next to your controlling area. Click the new entries button in the header. You will notice that the company code entry column in the assignment box is empty and ready for postings.

D. Assign number ranges to controlling area (KANK):

In this section, you will prefer the following tasks:

- Set up number range assignment group

- Assign activates as necessary

- Create number range intervals

There are two methods for creating your assignment groups: copy from an existing controlling area or create a new group from scratch. It is far easier to copy a group, so we recommend this approach. Any defaults carried over with the copied group can be augmented later. This augmentation would be necessary if you wanted a specific activity, like assessments, to post to a document number range other than the SAP default.

Set up number range assignment groups: Copy

In the CO area field, enter the ID of the controlling area to be copied.

Controlling area 0001 is delivered with the system and can be used to copy.

Click the copy as icon.

In the box, enter the name of the receiving controlling area and press enter. If the copy was successful, you will receive a message at the bottom of the screen that reads "CO Area 0001 copied to XXXX", when XXXX refers to the recipient controlling area.

To maintain your number range groups, select the group maintain icon on the number ranges for CO document screen. To maintain number range croups screen appears. You will notice that all the activity assignments are copied from CO Area 0001.

To move an unassigned activity to a range group, place your cursor on the activity and choose the select element icon. You will notice that activity becomes highlighted.

Place a check next to the activity group to which you want the activity assigned. Select the element/ group button. The activity moves from the not assigned section to your new activity group. Repeat this assignment as often as necessary.

Set up number range assignment groups: manual

In the text field, enter the name of the new group.

Enter the number range that will support the new range group in from the number and to number fields. Be sure that the new number range does not overlap an existing range. SAP will do a check automatically. To view the existing number ranges, drop to the existing number ranges section and scroll using the + and – keys. When you are finished entering the number ranges, press enter. The insert box disappear and you are returned to the maintain number ranges screen.

Check number range status:
Enter a controlling area ID in the CO area field.
Select the maintain status icon found in the center of the screen. A list of the number intervals appears. From this list, you can reset any range to 0 or adjust the number to something more appropriate.

Once you are satisfied with the number range groups and number interval assignments, the controlling area number assignment process is complete.

Change the number range status:
Enter a controlling area ID in the CO Area field.

Select the maintain status icon found in the center of the screen. A list of the number intervals appears. From this list, you can reset any range to 0 or adjust the number to something more appropriate.

II. OPERATING CONCERN:

The operating concern is the main organizational unit within CO-PA. It is utilized as a management tool to analyze specific markets or business segments.

Maintain operating concern (KEA0/KEP8)
Maintain CO versions (OKEQ)

A. Maintain operating concern (KEA0):
Operating concern ID: Enter a four character alphanumeric concern.
Name of operating concern: Enter the description of you operating concern.

B. Maintain CO versions (OKEQ):

The maintain version configuration screen is divided into two sections: a navigation section and general version definition section. In the navigation sections there are six (6) areas to maintain:

General CO version
Settings for operating concern
Settings for profit center accounting
Settings in controlling area
Setting for fiscal year
Delta version —used ABC

To make the controlling area functional for version 0, you need to define the CO version and maintain activation for the fiscal year. Begin the process by setting the default controlling area:

Choose extràsà set CO area
Enter the controlling area ID you are maintaining

Because version 0 is generated within the controlling area, the settings for the fiscal year will be configured next. When version 0 is generated, SAP makes the version available for five years by default. Should need arise, additional years can be added once the last year expires.

Fiscal year version parameters:
To maintain the version parameters, select version 0min the general version definition section of the maintain version configuration screen. Scroll through the navigation section to step 5, settings for the fiscal year, using the page up/down buttons found in the middle of the screen. Select the details button icon next to the section and the fiscal year version parameters screen appears. Select new entries and a new fiscal year dependent version details screen appears.

Let's look at the fields in the fiscal version details screen:

Fiscal year: Enter the fiscal year for which you are maintaining the version. You will have to maintain a version for each year.

Version blocked: If this field is active, planning is locked. This setting is useful if you want to freeze plan values after a certain data.

Planning integration: Activate this field if you want to transfer plan data from cost centers to profit center accounting or to special ledgers. Although no plan data exists in this version yet, you can change this setting. If plan data has been posted, the integration indicators can be activated through transaction KP96: activate line items and planning integration. Once this field is activated, SAP posts previously planned line items.

Copying allowed: Select this field if you want to copy plan version to one another. We recommend that you activate the settings because of the flexibility it adds to your planning capabilities. With copying allowed activated, a company could easily maintain multiple planning scenarios, copying the information from one to another and then making version—specific changes. Upon completion and approval of the plan, the final version could quickly be copied back to version 0 and used in reporting and analysis.

Exchange type: Enter the key for how you will store exchange rates in the exchange type system.P-standard transaction for cost planning- is used most frequently.

Value set: Enter a data in the value set field if you want the same data used for all planning translations. If this field is left blank, SAP will determine the exchange rate on a period-by-period basis. Leave this blank if you want SAP to track any exchange rate fluctuations.

Planning integration with CCA: This field refers to integration with internal orders and WBS elements. If this field is activated, any planned order settlements will be picked up in cost center accounting. In addition, any planned assessments, distributions, or indirect activity allocations from cost centers to orders/WBS elements will be permitted. Also, if planning integration with CCA is activated, integration could occur between order/WBS elements and PCA and /or special ledgers.

Valuation version for IAA: IAA stands for indirect activity allocation. This field can be set only if planning integration with CCA is inactive. The default version from SAP is 0.

Pure iterative price: This field should be activated if you wish to maintain parallel activity prices within one version. The requirement for activation is that you must manually ser the allocation prices during your activity type planning. If this field is not activated, SAP only calculates the prices resulting from your activity planning.

Plan method: Use this field to choose a method for activity price planning, SAP provides three methods: periodic, average, and cumulative.

Actual method: Similar to plan method, use actual method to choose the type of activity for price calculations. SDP offers three types of activity price calculations—periodic, average, and cumulative.

Revaluation: Use this field to determine whether actual activities are revaluated or not. If it's checked, you can determine whether actual activity is revaluated using only an actual price or both the actual and the planned price.

Cost component lay-out: If activity pricing is used in product costing or cost center accounting and you are using a cost component lay-out, enter the desired lay-out key in the cost component lay-out box.

Profit center accounting version parameters:
While in the CO versions change maintenance transactions OKEQ, select the version you wish to maintain and choose settings for profit center accounting. The ECPCA fiscal year dependent version parameters screen appears.

Select new entries. In the version parameters box, three are several fields to complete:

Fiscal year: Enter the fiscal year for which the settings are valid.

Version locked: Activate version locked if the version should be protected from entries or changes.

Online data transfer: If this field is activated, all transactions will update PCA automatically. If it's not activated, postings will have to be transferred manually through special transactions.

Line item: Activate line items if you want to use line item postings for all planning transactions. When finished, save your settings. That screen concludes the version maintenance for now.

Summary of controlling enterprise structure:
I. The controlling area
- àControlling area definition
- àActivate component/control indicators
- àAssign company codes to controlling area
- àAssign number ranges to controlling area

II. The operating concern
- àOperating concern definition
- àMaintain CO versions

CONTROLLING:

Features of controlling:
- Cost center accounting
- Internal order
- Profit center accounting
- Product cost controlling (CO-PC)
- Profitability analysis (CO-PA)

Controlling organizational set-up:

a) Maintain controlling area (OKKP):

Spro/img/controlling/general controlling/organization/maintain controlling area
Double click on maintain controlling area.
Go to new entries
Controlling area   : 1116
Name   : controlling area for TISCO
Person responsible   : ACCOUNTANT1
Company code—controlling area: controlling area same as company code
Currency type   : 10
Currency   : INR
Chart of accounts   : 1116
Fiscal year variant   : V3
Cost center standard hierarchy: TISCO_HIER

Save

System gives message: Standard hierarchy TISCO_HIER does not exist. Should system TISCO_HIER be created as a standard hierarchy? Say "yes'

Double click on activate components/control indicators.

Go to new entries
Controlling area   : 1116
Fiscal year   : 2006
Cost centers   : component active
Select Activity Type
Order management   : component active
Select Profit center.
Select all currencies.
Save.
System gives message: critical transport: control indicator in controlling area.
Double click on assignment of company code
Go to new entries
Company code   : 1116
Save.

b) Maintain number ranges for controlling documents (KANK):

Spro/img/controlling/general controlling/organization/maintain number ranges for controlling documents.
Give controlling area   : 1116
Select maintain groups
Select group on menu bar
Select insert
Text   : controlling area for TISCO
From number   to number
1
1000
Enter
Select COIN –controlling through -postings from FI
Go to edit on menu bar
Select select element

Select RKIU
Go to edit

Select select element

Select RKP1
Go to edit
Select select element

Select RKP2
Go to edit
Select select element

Select RKP3
Go to edit
Select select element

Select RKPU
Go to edit
Select select element

Select RKU1
Go to edit
Select select element

Select RKU3
Go to edit
Select select element

Select controlling area for TISCO
Go to edit.
Select assign element group
Save.

c) Maintain CO versions (OKEQ):

Spro/img/controlling/general
controlling/organization/maintain versions

Version   : select 0(plan/actual version)
Double click on settings for each fiscal year
Controlling area   : 1116
Version   : 0
Enter

Go to new entries

Fiscal year   : 2006
Select integrated planning
Select copying allowed
Exchange rate type   : B
Save.

Question 02: Posting key and Field status group

What is the difference among Account group, posting key and Field status group in terms field status?

A: Account group defines:
- length of gl account number
- no. ranges of the gl account numbers
- Field status of the GL account master data in the company code segment (Which fields to appear when you create a gl account. To control: double click on your GL account group in Screen transaction code OBD4)

Posting key defines:
- Whether the line item is a debit or credit
- To which type of account the amount should be posted to (ex: when you use posting key 40, you will be able to post to gl accounts. When you use posting key 01, you will be only able to post to customer account.
- Document screen layout during posting of a document. (Which fields to appear in a document...double click on the posting key and select field status and make the entries as required /optional etc)

Field status group defines:

Document screen layout during posting of a document. (Which fields to appear in a document...double click on the field status group and select fields and make the entries as required /optional etc)

LOGIC: you assign field status variant to the company code, FSV is a bundle of field status groups.

Example: in FSG G001 you have made the text as required entry...you assigned the field status group g001 to cash account. so when you use cash account and try to post a document it will definitely prompt you to enter the text (text made as required.)

Both FSG and PK control the same fields in a document. There is no dominance between FSG and Posting keys. We should know the allowed combinations.

If text is made required in PK and suppressed in FSG, the system will issue an error message. Rules for PK and FSG are set incorrectly for SGTXT field.

Permissible combinations:

Pk	R/S	O/S	R/o	R	S	O
FSG	S/R	S/O	o/r	R	S	O
Result	e	SD	RD	NP	NP	NP

R= required
s= suppressed
e=error
SD= Suppressed dominates
Rd= required dominates
Np=no problem.

Question 03: Identify target cost version

How do I know which target cost version we are using?

A: To find out which version is used for your Target Cost, try this menu path:

IMG > Controlling -> Product Cost Controlling -> Cost Object Controlling -> Product Cost by Order -> Period-end Closing -> Variance Calculation -> Define Target Cost Versions (tcode OKV6).

Question 04: Parking of document

What is Parking of Document? What is the main purpose of this document? Why are we using this one in FI? How is it useful?

A: Parking documents is used when we need to get any clarification regarding some account. We can temporarily park or store this document till we get it cleared or approved.

Then we can post it.

Parking does not update the accounts, it just stores the document. Whereas posting will update the accounts (for example: the reducing/increasing of the account balances).

The TC for Parking Documents is F-02 -> enter the required details ->go to the menu (at top) ->Document-> Park.

To post a parked document: FBV0-> go to the menu Document-> Post.

Other TCs used pertaining to Parking of Documents:
FV50: Post / Delete: Single Screen Transaction
FBV2: Change
FBV3: Display
FBV4: Change Header
FBV5: Display Changes
FBV6: Refuse

Question 05: Low value assets

How can we define low value assets in SAP?

A: To define low value assets in SAP:

1. Create asset class separately for LVA.
2. Define deposit Key separately which must ensure that deposit is fully computed and post it to G/L Account.

Question 06: Creating Vendor Invoice

I created a Vendor and want to create a vendor invoice. I got this error message: "In company code 3000, the number range 19 is missing for the year 2006". How do I rectify this problem?

A: Try Document Types for Number Ranges (T. Code - OBA7) Under No (enter 19) year (2006) range (from -to) enter and save.

And then try and enter the Invoice Posting – Direct Invoices Enter Vendor Invoices Trans Code: F-43/Trans Code: FB60 (30 cr vendor acc, 40 debit expense acc).

Define Document Types (T. Code – OBA7):
Menu Path >SPRO >Financial Accounting >Financial Accounting Global Settings >Document > Document Header >Define Document Types >Click on Process Button

Every document contains a document type in its header data. This document type is defaulted when you are entering the document. If you do not agree with the default document type you can enter one yourself. The standard system is delivered with the following document types (amongst others).

Type	Description	Number Range
DR	Customer Invoice	18
DZ	Customer Payment	14
DG	Customer Credit Memo	16
KR	Vendor Invoice	19
KZ	Vendor Payment	15
KG	Vendor Credit Memo	17
AB	Accounting Document	01
SA	GL Accounting Document	01

Whatever the documents types are provided by SAP R/3 system are sufficient and they will meet your needs. So you do not need to create any document types on your own unless it is an industry specific organization or you have decided to create on your own, normally which comes in the Blue Print in the design stage.

Functions of the Document Types:

1. Sometimes, it is used to differentiate between business transactions. The document type tells you instantly what sort of a business transaction is in question. This is useful, for example when displaying line items.

2. It is also used in controlling the posting to accounts (vendor, customer and GL accounts). The document type determines which accounts that particular document can be posted to.

Issuing document numbers and controlling document storage: Every document type has a number range allocated to it from which the numbers for the SAP documents you create are taken. The original documents from one number range should be stored together. In this way, the document type controls document storage. The document type can also specify that the document should be posted using the net posting procedure.

Question 07: Bank Reconciliation Statement

What are the steps to make a BRS?

A: The following are the steps for BRS:

1. Create Bank Master Data - This can be created through T.Code FI01 or you can also create the house bank through IMG/FA/Bank accounting/Bank account

2. Define House Bank

3. Set up Bank selection payment program - IMG/FA/ARAP/BT/AUTOIP/PM/Bank selection for payment prg.

   a. setup all co codes for payment transaction - Customer and vendors

   b. setup paying co codes for payment transactions

   c. setup payment method per country

   d. setup payment method per co code for payment transaction

   e. setup bank determination for payment transaction

Please go for Check Management using T code FCHI: (IMG/FA/ARAP/BT/OP/AutoOp/PaymentMediaccountheckMa nagement) and for void reasons FCHV. You can create Bank Reconciliation statement by TC FF67: (SAP/AC/Treasury/CashManagement/Incomings/ManualBankS tatement). Don't forget to keep the opening Balance as zero. Use FBEA for post process.

Question 08: Document flow confusion

When posting a customer invoice, the sub ledger will be debited with that amount. Will the same amount be posted to the G/L only or the very same amount will also be posted to the reconciliation general ledger?

A: Customer and Vendor accounts are maintained in a sub ledger. Posting to these accounts will also be posted to the A/R and A/P reconciliation accounts. All reconciliation accounts are GL accounts but all G/L accounts are not reconciliation accounts.

There are thousands of customers/vendors in a large business. All these are personal accounts (there are three types of accounts: nominal, personal and real). These personal accounts are grouped in to sub-ledgers and any posting to them is reconciled to the G/L via the reconciliation accounts.

Personal accounts: Accounts in the name of individuals, organizations etc.
For example, Company A Account, XYZ limited co ACCOUNT, Suresh ACCOUNT, Indian Bank ACCOUNT, etc.

Real Accounts: These are accounts related to assets, both real and tangible.
For example, furniture account, machinery account, accounts receivables account, etc.

Nominal Accounts: These are related to incomes/expenditures and profit/losses.
For example, sales Account, salary account, etc.

All the Vendors are grouped under Accounts Payable & Customers are grouped under Accounts Receivable. And also always any time the balance in reconciliation account shows as zero.

Ex: Vendors transaction:
    For Invoice posting:
    Inventory Account   Dr
    To Vendor Account...............Accounts Payable Account
(Reconciliation Ledger)

In SAP since we are linking in the G/L Master Accounts Payable with the reconciliation accounts type setting as Vendors. Hence with one entry, 3 accounts are automatically updated.

Accounts Payable is Liability & Inventory is Current Assets.
     For Payment to Vendor:
     Vendor Account   Dr.....Accounts Payable Account
     To Bank/ Cash Account

Ex: Customer Transaction:
     Sales Invoice Posting:
     Customer Account   Dr...Accounts Receivable Account
(Reconciliation Account)

     To Sales Account
     Receipt Posting:
     Bank Account   Dr
     To Customer Account...........Accounts Receivable Account

In Normal Accounting the Reconciliation Accounts are called as Control Accounts and we pass 2 entries for each transaction i.e., Sale, as following:

  1) Customer Account   Dr (Sales Ledger / Accounts Receivable Account)
       To Sales Account   (General Ledger)
  2) Accounts Receivable Account   Dr (General Ledger)
       To Customer Account   (Sales Ledger Adjustment Account)

Hence, any time the Control Account balance is zero.

Question 09: Change reconciliation account of customer master

Can you change the account number in the vendor or customer master data?

A: There is no problem to change the account number in the vendor or customer master data, that is if:

All Document Items that were created in the old account will be posted in the same old account when you have a payment posting, compensations, etc.

All document created after the change will be posted in the new account as well as the payment postings, compensations and others.

The system will separate the postings in accordance with the moment at the documents were created.

You can do a test in the development client before you do the change in the production. For example: You can create a new reconciliation account because you want the G/L accounts to separate out sales. Just switched the setting in Customer Master and off you go. SAP will recognized the old account for the old postings and used the new account for any new postings.

Here is the official SAP help on the subject:
You should run balance sheet adjustment program after any reconciliation account change. The system performs any adjustments required due to the change of reconciliation accounts or G/L accounts. The items from the old reconciliation accounts are allocated to the new accounts.

Since you cannot post to the reconciliation accounts directly, the postings are made to temporary adjustment accounts.

These adjustment accounts should be displayed along with the relevant reconciliation account in the balance sheet. The postings are then reversed after the balance sheet has been created.

The program for sorting the payables and receivables makes the necessary adjustments automatically. This means that you have to define the adjustment account numbers and the posting keys for these postings in the system.

If you purchase and install the FI-LC Consolidation application and have bought up a previous customer or vendor (thus also taking on his/her payables and receivables), please refer to the note in the report documentation on changed reconciliation accounts. To define the account numbers, select the activity Define adjustment accounts for changed reconciliation accounts in the Accounts Receivable and Accounts Payable Implementation Guide.

You should only run this program if your new reconciliation account is classified differently from the original in your FS. e.g.. AR to Inter Company accounts. It will just reclassify the existing balance. The line items will not be transferred. If not, then no need to run the program at all.

Question 10: Various postings to GL account

What are the postings to the GL account and how does it take place?

A: During various postings, the GL account postings will be take place as follows:

For Domestic Procurement of Raw Material:
During GR

Material Stock	Dr.
GR/IR clearing	Cr.

During Excise Invoice Credit

Cenvat Account	Dr.
Cenvat Clearing	Cr.

During Invoice Verification

Cenvat Clearing	Dr.
GR/IR Clearing	Dr.
Vendor Payable	Cr.

For Domestic procurement of Capital Goods:
During GR

Material Stock	Dr.
GR/IR clearing	Cr.

During Excise Invoice Credit

Cenvat Account	Dr. (50%)
Cenvat On-hold	Dr. (50%)
Cenvat Clearing	Cr.

During Invoice Verification

Cenvat Clearing	Dr.
GR/IR Clearing	Dr.
Vendor Payable	Cr.

Subsequent of Capital Goods

Cenvat Account	Dr. (50%)
Cenvat On-hold	Cr. (50%)

For Import Procurement of Raw Material:
During Customs Duty Clearing invoice

Custom Clearing	Dr.

	Custom Payable	Cr.
During GR		
	Material Stock	Dr.
	GR/IR clearing	Cr.
During Excise Invoice Credit		
	Cenvat Account	Dr.
	Custom Clearing	Cr.
During Invoice Verification		
	GR/IR Clearing	Dr.
	Vendor Payable	Cr.

For Excise Duty Credit of Raw Material without PO:

Cenvat Account	Dr.
Cenvat Clearing	Cr.

For Excise Duty Reversal through Excise JV:

Cenvat Clearing	Dr.
Cenvat Account	Cr.

During Excise Invoice Creation
Cenvat Suspense Account	Dr.
Cenvat payable	Cr.

For TR6C Challan:
PLA Account	Dr.
PLA on hold Account	Cr.

During Fortnightly Utilization
Cenvat payable	Dr.
Cenvat Account	Cr.
PLA Account	Cr.

Question 11: Creating new company code

What are the checklists of items to set up when creating a new company code in an existing system?

A: The checklists for creating a new company code as follows:

Edit delete company code
Assign company code to chart of accounts OB62
Assign company code to Fiscal year variant OB37
Assign company code to posting period variant
Document number ranges copy from 0300 company code
Enable Fiscal year variant default
Enable default value date
Assign company code to field status variant
Screen variants for document entry
Define tolerance groups for employees OBA4
Define validations for posting OB28
Define Substitution in accounting documents OBBH
Maximum Exchange rate difference
Enter global Parameters
Define Additional local currencies
Define company
Assign company code to company
Copy GL Accounts from the chart of accounts OBY2
Define Tolerance groups for GL accounts OBA0
Company code to credit control area
Company code to controlling area OX19
Global Company Code CoCde OB72
Substitution in Accounting Documents OBBZ
Customer / Vendor tolerances OBA3
Payment Program OBVU
Bank Accounts OBVCU
Tolerance Limits OMR6
Tax non taxable transactions OBCL
Assign company code to chart of depreciation OAOB
Payment program configuration OBZ1
Maintain Payment program configuration OBZ2
Tax default invoice verification OMR2

Question 12: APC

What is APC in assets?

A: APC is acquisition and production cost.

As a result of the integration in the R/3 System, Asset Accounting (FI-AA) transfers data directly to and from other R/3 components. For example, it is possible to post from the Materials Management (MM) component directly to FI-AA. When an asset is purchased or produced in-house, you can directly post the invoice receipt or goods receipt, or the withdrawal from the warehouse, to assets in the Asset Accounting component. At the same time, you can pass on depreciation and interest directly to the Financial Accounting (FI) and Controlling (CO) components. From the Plant Maintenance (PM) component, you can settle maintenance activities that require capitalization to assets

If you post to an asset when entering a purchase requisition or an outline agreement, the system checks, with reference to the planned delivery date whether the fixed asset actually exists and whether you can post to it. The same checks are carried out if you post to a fixed asset when entering a purchase order. Moreover, the system ensures that you do not exceed the upper limit for low-value assets. You can still change the asset, for which account assignment is to be performed, until receipt of the first goods or invoice for a purchase order.

If you want to carry out account assignment to assets when creating purchase orders, purchase requisitions and outline agreements, the account entered in Financial Accounting for "Acquisition and production costs" must be assigned to a field status group that allows entries in the field groups "asset number/sub-number," "transaction type," and "quantity."

Question 13: Cost center

How do you create new cost center?

A: To create cost center:

Create Cost Center (T. Code – KS01)

Enter Cost Center Name, Validity date
Press enter key

Please make sure that you select from the list AND do not select numeric values, only characteristics values can be selected.

Enter cost center name and description
Person responsible (optional)
Department
Cost center category (SELECT FROM THE LIST)
Hierarchy area (will be displayed automatically)
Business area
Currency

Note that cost center should be assigned to the lowest node on the standard hierarchy, if you attempt to enter master at summary level, SAP will stop the assignment with an error.

Question 14: Middle of the year Asset data transfer

I am transferring legacy asset data into SAP system in the middle of the year (30.06.2004). In the customization, I have maintained the asset take over date as 30.06.2004. And while I am creating the legacy asset through AS91, I am entering accumulated depreciation up to 30.06.2004. After creating this asset and when I checked the asset details at AW01N and in other reports, it is again calculating the depreciation for the 3 months. My fiscal year starts on 01.04.2004.

What did I miss in my configuration?

A: Verify your configuration settings:

1) Verify SPRO setting "period in which depreciation was posted" (Tr.Code: OAYC) and make sure the setting is 2004 and period is 3.

2) Verify whether you have given any special Fiscal year setting at SPRO. Asset Accounting-->Valuation--> Fiscal year--> Fiscal year Variant--> Specify other versions at the Company Code level.

If there is a separate fiscal year version for Asset Accounting, you have to review the problem from that perspective.

Your problem revolves around these two aspects only.

Question 15: Error as T880

I am using 4.7 version of SAP and while assigning company code, I am getting an error "T880". The company which I had defined shows it does not exist and continue with the error "T880".

How do I correct this error?

A: Try the following procedure:

1. To define a company:

Go to T.Code OX15

Click on New Entries
Company: 4 character Alph numeric key ex: ABCD
Provide Company Name: ABCD Company

Under Detailed info tab:

Provide company details like address, etc...
Country: Two character code XX
Language XX Currency XX
Then click on SAVE button.

Company is created.

2. To define company code:

T.Code OX02

Click New Entries

Company Code: 4 char name ex: ABCD
Company code name

SAVE

Company Edit Address Details

Title: Company

Name: EFGH
SAVE

3. Assessing Company Code to Company:

\nspr --> click on Enterprise structure --> Assign --> Financial Accounting assignment --> Assign Company code to company.

Click positions ex: DCBA
Click Enter
SAVE

The DCBA company code will be assigned to ABCD Company.

Question 16: House Banking

What is the procedure for house banking configuration?

A: Here is one possible House Banking configuration. The sample steps are as follows:

1. Creation of General Ledger Account iV SBI Current Account under Current Assets.
2. Creation of House Bank and assigning General Ledger Account # in House Bank.
3. Creation of Check Lots.
4. Purchase Invoice Posting.
5. Payment posting through bank and Clearing Party Account.
6. Manual check updating.
7. Check registers display.

Step 01: Creation of General Ledger Account iV SBI Current Account under Current Assets
FS00>VBCF>200101>WITH TEMLATE
BUTTON>200100>VBCH>SBI
CURRENT ACCOUNT- DESCRIPTION>SELECT
CREATE/BANK/INTEREST TAB> FIELD STATUS (G0005) iV
BANK>SAVE

Step 02: Creation of House Bank and assigning General Ledger Account # in House Bank
SPRO>FA>BANK ACCOUNTING>BANK ACCOUNTS>DEFINE HOUSE BANKS
TRANSACTION CODE: FI 12
„« VBCF>SELECT NEW ENTRIES BUTTON>USE HOUSE BANK NAME: SBI> BANK COUNTRY: IN>
„« BANK KEY: 1234 iV MANDATORY
„« TELEPHONE & ADDRESS
„« SAVE
„« SELECT CHANGE BUTTON
„« STATE BANK OF INDIA, ADDRESS
„« ENTER
„« SAVE
„« DOUBLE CLICK BANK ACCOUNTS
„« SELECT NEW ENTRIES
„« SBI 1 iV ACCOUNT ID

„« SBI CURRENT ACCOUNT 1 iV DISCRIPTION
„« BANK ACCOUNT NO. 67890
„« CURRENCY iV INR
„« GL ACCOUNT NO. 200101
„« SAVE

Step 03: Creation of Check Lots
ACCOUNTING> FA>ACCOUNTS PAYABLE>PERIODIC
PROCESSING>PAYMENTS
TRANSACTION CODE: F-110
„« FROM MENU SELECT ENVIRONMENT>CHECK
INFORMATION
„« NO.RANGES
„« TRANSACTION CODE: FCHI
„« VBCF>HOUSEBANK: SBI
„« SELECT CHANGE BUTTON
„« SELECT CREATE BUTTON
„« LOT NO.1
„« CHECK NO. 100000 TO 100100
„« SELECT NON-SEQUENTIAL (ANY CHEQUE ANY TIME)
„« SHORT INFORMATION: SBI
„« PURCHASE DATE/CHEQUE BOOK INTEREST DATE 01-07-
04
„« ENTER
„« SAVE

Step 04: To see the purchase posting
TC iV FBL1N
VENDOR ACCOUNT NO. 5200001
VBCF>SELECT OPEN ITEMS>OPEN KEY DATE: 01-07-
04>EXECUTE

Step 05: Payment posting through bank and Clearing Party
Account
ACCOUNTING>FA>ACCOUNTS PAYABLE>DOCUMENT
ENTRY>OUTGOING
PAYMENTS>POST
TRANSACTION CODE iV F-53
>01-07-2004>01-07-2004>KZ>VBCF
> ACCOUNT NO.200101 >BUSINESSAREA>VBCH
>TEXT: OUTGOING PAYMENT

>5200001 VENDOR ACCOUNT NO>SELECT PROCESS OPEN
ITEMS
BUTTON> DOUBLE CLICK THE PAYABLE AMOUNT>
DOCUMENT
Simulate and Save

GO AND SEE VENDOR ACCOUNT iV FBL1N
5200001>VBCF>SELECT CLEARED ITEMS > EXECUTE

Step 06: Manual Check Updation
ACCOUNTING>FA>ACCOUNTS
PAYABLE>ENVIRONMENT>CHECK
INFORMATION>CREATE>MANUAL CHECKS
TRANSACTION CODE: FCH5
„« GIVE THE CHECK NUMBER iV 100050
„« SAVE

Step 07: Check register display
ACCOUNTING>FA>ACCOUNTS
PAYABLE>ENVIRONMENT>CHECK
INFORMATION>DISPLAY>CHECK REGISTER
TRANSACTION CODE: FCHN
VBCF>EXECUTVE>DOUBLE CLICK ANY WHERE ON THE
LINE
ITEM>SELECT ACCOMPANYING DOCUMENT BUTTON IT
GIVES
AGAINST DETAILS

For check encashment date:
ACCOUNTING>FA>ACCOUNTSPAYABLE>ENVIRONMENT>C
HECK
INFORMATION>CHANGE>ADDITIONAL INFO/CASH
TRANSACTION CODE: FCH6
„« VBCF iV PAYING COMPANY CODE
„« SBI iV HOUSE BANK
„« SBI 1 iV ACCOUNT ID
„« 100050 iV CHECK NO.
„« ENTER
„« CHECK iV 5-07-04 iV ENCASHMENT DATE
„« SAVE
„« GO AND SEE THE CHECK REGISTER

„« FCHN iV TRANSACTION CODE
„« VBCF
„« EXECUTE

For unissued checks cancellation:
ACCOUNTING>FA>ACCOUNTS
PAYABLE>ENVIRONMENT>CHECK
INFORAMTION>VOID>UNISSUED CHECKS
TC _ FCH3
>VBCF>SBI>SBI 1
>100001
> VOID REASON CODE: 06 iV DESTROYED / UNUSED
> SELECT VOID BUTTON
IT GIVES 100101 TO 100101 VOIDES

GO AND CHECK THE CHECK REGISTER
FCHN
VBCF
EXECUTE
KEEP THE CURSOR ON CHECK NO. FROM TO
SELECT SORT IN ASCENDING ORDER BUTTON

To create check void reason code:
SPRO>FA>ARAP>BT>OUTGOINGPAYMENTS>AUTOMATICO
UTGOINGPAYMENTS>PAYMENT
MEDIA>CHECK MANAGEMENT>DEFINE VOID REASON
CODE
FCHV iV TC
„« SELECT NEW ENTRIES
„« CODE 20 (MAX. 2 DIGITS)
„« STOP PAYMENT FOR VBCF iV DISCRIPTION
„« SAVE

For checks cancellation:
„X PURCHASE INVOICE POSTING
„X PAYMENT POSTING THROUGH BANK AND CLEARING
VENDOR
ACCOUNT iV F-53
„X MANUAL CHECK UPDATION iV FCH5
„X CHECK REGISTER DISPLAY iV FCHN
„X ISSUE CHECK CANCELLATION

o RESET
o REVERSE
o CANCEL CHECK

For purchase invoice posting:
ACCOUNT iV F-43
03-07-2004>03-07-
2004>KR>VBCF>INR>31>5200001>ENTER>9999
AMT>VBCH>PURCHASEINVOICE POSTING-
TEXT>40>200100 (INV
RAW)>ENTER>*>VBCH>+>DOCUMENT
Simulate and Save

For Payment posting through bank and clearing vendor:
ACCOUNT iV F-53
03-07-2004>03-07-2004>KZ>VBCF>INR>BANK
ACCNO.200101>AMT>9999>VBCH>OUTGOING PAYMENT-
TEXT>
VENDOR ACCTNO.5200001>SELECT PROCESS OPEN
ITEMS>DOUBLE
CLICK PAYABLE AMOUNT 9999> DOCUMENT
Simulate and Save

For manual check updation:
ACCOUNT iV FCH5
AUTOMATICALLY>SBI>SBI1>100005>SAVE
CHECK REGISTER DISPLAY iV FCHN iV VBCF>EXECUTE

To issue check cancellation:
ACCOUNTING>FA>AP>ENVIRONMENT>CHECK
INFORMATION>VOID>CANCEL PAYMENT
TC iV FCH8
„« PAYING CO.CODE iV VBCF
„« SBI
„« SBI1
„« CHECK NO.100005 (which is to be cancelled)
„« VOID REASON CODE iV 20 iV STOP PAYMENT
„« GIVE REVERSAL REASON iV 01 iV REVERSE IN THE
CURRENT PERIOD
„« SELECT CANCEL PAYMENT BUTTON

„« MESSAGE CONFIRMATION
„« VERIFICATION THROUGH TC iV FCHN
„« VBCF>EXECUTE
„« VENDOR ACCOUNT iV FBL1N
„« 5200001>VBCF>SELECT OPEN ITEMS>KEY DATE 03-07-04 >
EXECUTE

To reissue of unissued voided check iV Check No. 100001:
ACCOUNTING>FA>AP>ENVIRONMENT>CHECKINFORMATION>DELETE>VOIDED
CHECKS
TC iV FCHE
VBCF>SBI>SBI1>CH.NO.100001>EXECUTE > YES FOR THE MESSAGE
„« SEE THE CHECK REGISTER iV FCHN>VBCF>EXECUTE

For terms of payment creation:
SPRO>FA>ARAP>BT>INCOMING
INVOICE/CREDITMEMOS>MAINTAIN
TERMS OF PAYMENT
NO TC
„« SELECT NEW ENTRIES BUTTON
„« PAYMENT TERMS iV VBC1
„« SELECT VENDOR AND CUSTOMER
„« SHORT TEXT iV WITH 10 iV 2%, 20 iV 1%, DUE -30
„« DEFAULT FOR BASELINE DATE
„« DOCUMENT DATE- BILL DATE
„« POSTING DATE iV GOODS RECEIPT DATE
„« ENTRY DATE iV QUALITY APPROVAL DATE
„« NO DEFAULT
„« SELECT POSTING DATE FOR DEFUALT FOR BASELINE
„« PAYMENT TERMS 2% 10 DAYS,1% 20 DAYS, 30 DAYS
„« ENTER
„« SYSTEM CREATES TEXT AUTOMATICALLY
„« SAVE
For Cash discounts received:

1. Creation of General Ledger Account, Cash Discount received
under other income group:
FS00
300100>VBCF>SELECTWITH TEMPLATE

BUTTON>400100>VBCF>ENTER>OTHER INCOME>PROFIT
AND LOSS
ACCOUNT>CASH DISCOUNT>CASH DISCOUNT RECD>SAVE

2. Assignment of cash discount received account for automatic
posting:
SPRO>FA>ARAP>BT>OUTGOING PAYMENTS>OUTGOING
PAYMENTS
GLOBAL SETTINGS> DEFINE ACCOUNTS FOR CASH
DISCOUNTS
TAKEN
TC- OBXU
„« CHART OF ACCOUNTS iV VBCF
„« ENTER
„« SAVE
„« GIVE THE ACCOUNT NO. 300100
„« SAVE

For Purchase Invoice Posting iV F-43:
03-07-04>03-07-
04>KR>VBCF>INR>31>5200001>ENTER>100000
AMT>PAYMENT TERMS: VBC1 (STOP
PAYMENT)>PURCHASE INVOICE
POSTING iV
TEXT>40>200120>ENTER>*>VBCH>+>DOCUMENT
Simulate and Save

For outgoing payment iV F-53:
03-07-04>03-07-04>KZ>VBCF>INR>200101BANK
ACCT>98000AMT>VBCH>OUTGOING PAYMENT
TEXT>SELECT
PROCESS OPEN ITEMS BUTTON>DOUBLE CLICK AGAINST
PAYABLE
AMOUNT>DOCUMENT SIMULATE >DOUBLE CLICK BLUE
FONT LINE
ITEM>+ AT TEXT>SAVE

Question 17: Interest calculation

What is the procedure to run the bank interest calculation ?

A: There are two defined interest calculation types in the SAP system.

1. Balance interest calculation.
2. Item interest calculation.

System defined variant for balance interest calculation type is 'S' and item interest calculation type is 'P'. Balance interest type calculation is used for G L Accounts. Item interest type calculation is used for vendors and customers.

To display all transaction codes:
   Go to t.code:SE16
   Table name: TSTC
   Keep blank maximum number of hits.
   Total transaction codes in SAP 70837.

The following steps are involved in interest calculation.
1. Define interest calculation types (OB46)
2. Prepare account balance interest calculation (OBAA)
3. Define reference interest rate (OBAC)
4. Define time dependent terms (OB81)
5. Enter interest values (OB83)
6. Creation of G L Accounts (FS00)
7. Define automatic posting (OBV2)
8. Entry for loan (F-02)
9. Interest calculation run (F.52)

Step 01: Define interest calculation types (OB46):
Spro/img/financial accounting/G L Accounting/business transactions/bank ACCOUNT interest calculation/interest calculation global settings/define interest calculation types.

   Go to new entries

Interest Id calculation type	Name	Interest

V1	balance interest type	S
V2	item interest type	P
Save		

Step 02: Prepare account balance interest calculation (OBAA):
Spro/img/financial accounting/GL Accounting/business transactions/bank account interest calculations/interest calculation global settings/prepare account balance interest calculation.

Go to new entries
Give calculation indicator   : V1
Interest calculation frequency   : 01
Calendar type   : G (28, 29, 30, 31)
Give number range   : 03
Select balance plus interest.
Save

Go to new entries.
Calculation indicator   : V2
Interest calculation frequency   : 01
Calendar type   : G
Number range   : 03
Select balance +interest
Save

Step 03: Define reference interest rate (OBAC):
Spro/img/financial accounting/G L Accounting/business transactions/bank account interest calculation/interest calculation/define reference interest rates.
Go to new entries
Reference interest rate   : V1
Long text   : 12%balanace
interest
Short text   : 12% balance
interest
Date from   : 1.4.2006
Currency   : Inr
Save

Go to new entries F8
Reference interest rate   : V2
Long text   : 15% item interest

Short text   : 15%item interest
Date from   : 1.4.2006
Currency   : Inr
Save

Step 04: Define time dependent terms (OB81):
Spro/img/financial accounting/ G L Accounting/business
transactions/bank account interest calculation/interest
calculation/define time dependent terms.

Go to new entries
Interest calculation indicator   : V1
Currency key   : Inr
Effective from   : 1.4.2006
Sequential no   : 01
Term   : debit interest
balance interest calculation
Reference interest rate   : V1
Save

Go to new entries or f8
Interest calculation indicator   : V1
Currency   : Inr
Effective from   : 1.4.2006
Sequential no   : 02
Term   : credit interest
balance interest calculation
Reference interest rate   : V1
Save

Go to new entry or f8
Interest cal. Indicator   : V2
Currency   : Inr
Effective from   : 1.4.2006
Sequential no   : 01
Term   : debit interest
arrears interest calculation
Reference rate   : V2
Save

Go to new entry or f8
Interest cal. Indicator   : V2
Currency   : Inr
Effective from   : 1.4.2005

Sequential from   : 02
Term   : credit interest
arrears interest calculation
 Reference rate   : V2
 Save

Step 05: Enter Reference Interest Rate Values (OB83):
Spro/img/financial accounting/G L Accounting/business
transactions/bank ACCOUNT interest calculation/interest
calculation/enter interest values.

Go to new entries
Reference int. rate values effective from interest
rate
V1   1.4.2006   12
V2   1.4.2006   15
Save

Go to T.Code:OBD4 to create secured loans account group.
Go to new entries

Chart of accounts	account group	name	from
account to account			
1116	SELO	secured loans	100300
100399			
1116	INTR	interest	400100
400199			
Save			

Step 06: Creation of G L Accounts (FS00):
 G L ACCOUNT no   : 100305
 Company code   : 1116
 Select create button
 Account group   : secured loans
 Select balance sheet account
 Short text   :IB O D Account
 Long text   :Indian bank overdraft
account

 Select control data tab
 Select only balances in local currencies
 Select open item
 Select line item display
 Sort key   : 002

Select create/bank/interest tab
Field status group   : G005
Select relevant to cash flow
Interest calculation indicator : V1
Save

Give G L ACCOUNT no   : 400105
Company code   : 1116
Select create button
Account group   : interest
Select profit and loss account
Short text   : interest on O D Account
Long text   : interest on O D Account

Select control data tab.
Select only balances in local currencies
Select line item display
Sort key   : 002

Select create/bank/interest tab
Field status group   : G001
Save

Step 07: Define automatic posting account (OBV2):
Spro/img/financial accounting/G L Accounting/business
transactions/bank ACCOUNT interest calculations/interest
posting/prepare G L ACCOUNT balance interest calculation

Go to accounts
Chart of accounts   : 1116

ACCOUNT symbol	currency	G L ACCOUNT
0002	Inr	400105(interest on o d account)
2000	Inr	100305(I B o d account)

Save

Step 08: Entry for loan (F-02):
Give document date   : 1.4.2006
Posting date   : 1.4.2006

Type   : SA
Company code   : 1116
Currency   : INR
Posting key   : 40
G L Account   : 200005(Indian bank account)
Enter
Amount   : 2500000
Business area   : TISC
Value date   : 16.07.2006
Text   : loan received
Posting key   : 50
G L Account   : 100305(bank of Baroda O D account)
Enter
Amount   : *
Business area   : TISC
Text   : +
Save

Step 09: Interest calculation run (F.52):
Accounting/financial accounting/general ledger/periodic processing/interest calculation/balances

Give chart of accounts   : 1116
G L ACCOUNT no   : 100305(bank o d account)
Company code   : 1116
Calculation period   : 1.7.2006 to 31.7.2007
Select leap year.
Select post also if value date in past
Select update master records
Execute

Go to system on menu bar.
Select services
Select batch input
Select sessions
Select RFSZIS00
Select process
Select display errors only
Again select process

The system gives the message: "processing of batch input session completed";

Question 18: Electronic Bank Statement

What is the procedure for customizing an Electronic Bank Reconciliation statement?

A: To set up Electronic Bank Statements (Processing in SAP for most customers in North America):

1. Create House Bank and Account ID (FI12)

2. Setup EDI Partner Profile for FINSTA Message Type (WE20)

3. Configure Global Settings for EBS (IMG)

  - Create Account Symbols
  - Assign Accounts to Account Symbols
  - Create Keys for Posting Rules
  - Define Posting Rules
  - Create Transaction Types
  - Assign External Transaction Types to Posting Rules
  - Assign Bank Accounts to Transaction Types

4. Define Search String for EBS (Optional)
  - Search String Definition
  - Search String Use

5. Define Program and Variant Selection

Additional information is also available in the SAP Library under:
Financial Accounting > Bank Accounting (FI-BL) > Electronic Bank Statement
>Electronic Account Statement Customizing

SAP R/3 FICO Tcodes

Currency Conversion

Question 19: Convert in update rules

We need to follow SAP standards to maintain currency translation type and also loading exchange rate using flat file. In the ODS, we will be having the Amount Key Figure in local currency but data in Info Cube will be stored in USD. How can I do this?

A: Create another key figure with fix currency USD and convert in update rules with the following code:

```
CALL FUNCTION 'CONVERT_TO_FOREIGN_CURRENCY'
EXPORTING
DATE = COMM_STRUCTURE-[date for exchange rate]
FOREIGN_CURRENCY = 'USD'
LOCAL_AMOUNT = COMM_STRUCTURE-/bic/zsellvdoc
LOCAL_CURRENCY = COMM_STRUCTURE-[currency used]
IMPORTING
FOREIGN_AMOUNT = RESULT
EXCEPTIONS
NO_RATE_FOUND = 1
OVERFLOW = 2
NO_FACTORS_FOUND = 3
NO_SPREAD_FOUND = 4
DERIVED_2_TIMES = 5
OTHERS = 6.
IF SY-SUBRC <> 0.
RESULT = 0.
END IF
```

Question 20: Start routine

We have the three different types of currencies in the transaction data for oPO_VALUE. I read from the documentation that we can do the currency translation at three places, either at Bex, update rules or transfer rules. How can I write a routine in transfer rules for currency conversion?

A: I have used this in the Update Rule start Routine. When you get into the Update Rule maintenance, you can see a button for maintaining the Start Routine.

The outline of the code looks like this:

```
data: CMP1CONV type f,
S_AMT_1 type f,
CALMONTH like rsgeneral-chavl.
...

Move DATA_PACKAGE-/BIC/CMP1PRICE to S_AMT_1.
CALL FUNCTION 'RSW_CURRENCY_TRANSLATION'
EXPORTING
I_CTTNM = 'ANYCALMON'
I_AMOUNT = S_AMT_1
I_SCUR = DATA_PACKAGE-/BIC/CMP_CURR1
I_TCUR = I_OPP_NUM-CRM_CURREN
I_TIME_IOBJVL = CALMONTH
IMPORTING
E_AMOUNT = CMP1CONV
E_TCUR = I_OPP_NUM-CRM_CURREN
```

Try to look at some other start routine in the system (if available). It will help to give you an idea of where and how the code goes in.

Question 21: Currency conversion

My report must consist of currency field and the currency unit must be in dollars. The net value must be converted from EURO to USD. How can I convert the value of EURO to the USD considering the currency value varies from time to time?

A: Try this function module:

"CONVERT_TO_FOREIGN_CURRENCY" – This translates local currency amount into foreign currency.

An amount in foreign currency is calculated from a specified local currency amount. You may either specify the translation rate manually (Parameter RATE) or have the system determine it from table TCURR on the basis of the rate type, date and currency key. The ratios for the units of the currencies involved in the translation are significant for this translation, table TCURR is always read by the program and there must be a valid entry for the data specified. If exchange rate fixing is defined for exchange rate type TYPE_OF_RATE, or an alternative exchange rate type is defined for the currency pair, this information is transferred to the calling program.

When table TCURR is read, the foreign currency key is always taken as the first part of the key and the local currency as the second part. If this entry is not in the table, the key is re-read in reverse sequence.

Here's a sample code:

```
CALL FUNCTION 'CONVERT_TO_FOREIGN_CURRENCY'
EXPORTING DATE = BKPF-WWERT
FOREIGN_CURRENCY = BKPF-WAERS
LOCAL_CURRENCY = T001-WAERS
LOCAL_AMOUNT = BSEG-DMBTR
RATE = BKPF-KURSF
TYPE_OF_RATE = 'M'
IMPORTING EXCHANGE_RATE = KURS
FOREIGN_AMOUNT = BSEG-WRBTR
FOREIGN_FACTOR = FAKTOR-F
LOCAL_FACTOR = FAKTOR-L
EXCEPTIONS NO_RATE_FOUND = 4
```

NO_FACTORS_FOUND = 8.

Try this also and use the following F.M's:

CONVERT_TO_FOREIGN_CURRENCY - Converts local currency to foreign currency.

CONVERT_TO_LOCAL_CURRENCY - Converts from foreign currency to local currency

```
Code:
PARAMETERS: P_UKURS LIKE TCURR-UKURS.
DATA: BEGIN OF GI_TAB OCCURS 0,
KONWA LIKE KONP-KONWA,
STPRS LIKE MBEW-STPRS,
WAERS LIKE T001-WAERS,
END OF GI_TAB.

DATA: L_STPRS LIKE MBEW-STPRS,
L_RATE LIKE TCURR-UKURS.

IF P_UKURS IS INITIAL.
CLEAR L_RATE.
ELSE.
L_RATE = P_UKURS / 100.
ENDIF.


CALL FUNCTION 'CONVERT_TO_FOREIGN_CURRENCY'
EXPORTING
DATE = SY-DATUM
FOREIGN_CURRENCY = GI_TAB-KONWA
LOCAL_AMOUNT = GI_TAB-STPRS
LOCAL_CURRENCY = GI_TAB-WAERS
RATE = L_RATE
IMPORTING
FOREIGN_AMOUNT = L_STPRS
EXCEPTIONS
NO_RATE_FOUND = 1
OVERFLOW = 2
NO_FACTORS_FOUND = 3
NO_SPREAD_FOUND = 4
DERIVED_2_TIMES = 5
OTHERS = 6.
```

```
CALL FUNCTION 'CONVERT_TO_LOCAL_CURRENCY'
EXPORTING
DATE = SY-DATUM
FOREIGN_AMOUNT = L_BELOEB
FOREIGN_CURRENCY = 'JPY'
LOCAL_CURRENCY = 'DKK'
RATE = L_RATE
* TYPE_OF_RATE = 'M'
IMPORTING
EXCHANGE_RATE = L_RATE
* FOREIGN_FACTOR =
LOCAL_AMOUNT = L_BELOEB
* LOCAL_FACTOR =
* EXCHANGE_RATEX =
* FIXED_RATE =
* DERIVED_RATE_TYPE =
EXCEPTIONS
NO_RATE_FOUND = 1
OVERFLOW = 2
NO_FACTORS_FOUND = 3
NO_SPREAD_FOUND = 4
DERIVED_2_TIMES = 5
OTHERS = 6.
```

Question 22: Foreign currency valuation

I need a foreign currency assessment at the end of the year to maintain our accounts at par with the changes that occurred on the foreign currency from a particular day. Is there a way to do this?

A: The following is the procedure to evaluate foreign exchange currency at the year end.

1. Check exchange rate types T. Code: OB07

Configure the exchange types for bank buying and bank selling transactions, generally there are three types of exchange types:

B Type: Std. conversion at bank selling (this is used to payment to vendors against to purchases).

G Type: Std. conversion for Bank buying (this is used for receipts from customers against sales /exports).

M type: this is the average method.

2. Define transaction rates for currency transactions T. Code: OBBS

This method of conversion is maintained at client level. Give the data that is converted from which currency to which currency and the conversion ratio between two currencies.

3. Enter exchange rates T. Code: OB08 or S_BCE_68000174 (for end user).
Here, you have to enter the rates of currencies like USD or INR on a particular date.

4. Enter default exchange rate types T. Code: OBA7 then go to document type SA and select exchange rate type for forex currency = B.

Doc type SA   ------ B type currency
Doc type RE/KR ------ B type currency

Doc type RV/DR ------ G type currency

5. Creation of general ledger accounts for posting of exchange gain and loss.
T. Code: FS00
Exchange Gain Account ---- Other Income group
Exchange Loss Account ---- Administrative Expenses Group

6. Prepare automatic postings for foreign currency valuation T. Code: OBA1
Select exchange rate difference using exchange rate key: KDB
Give the exchange rate Key, Gain account and Loss Account

7. Foreign currency valuation T. Code: F.05
Select vendors valuate check box and give the Vendor nos.
Select customer valuate check box and give the Customer nos.
Select G/L account check box and give the loan account nos. if any.

Execute the settings.

Question 23: Currency conversion dependent on date

I am displaying cumulative amount and want the amount to be converted in some currency. Now, when I convert the currency, the currency translation is done with rate on current date but I want that in cumulative amount. The currency translation should be done depending on that month's conversion rate.

I cannot change update rule right now because we already have several months' data in our infocubes. If I would change, then I will have to upload all the data again and that would take around a week's time. In some cases, BW downtime would be required.

We already have currency keys and currency rates maintained. When I am viewing data from Jan-May and say some KF cumulative value is 5000 and current rate of conversion is 10, then I would get 50000 but if for Jan. the conversion rate was 5 then 50000 would be wrong. It should be like this:

1000 * 5 = 5000
1000 * 10 = 10000
1000 * 10 = 10000
1000 * 10 = 10000
1000 * 10 = 10000

That would sum up to 45000 so there is a difference of 5000. How do I achieve what I need?

A: The Currency Key has a defined Exchange Rate. The Exchange Rate is Time Dependent. So you can mention the Date Range for the Particular Value for the Currencies.

You can set this in:

SPRO--> General Settings --> Currencies --> Enter Exchange Rates

Question 24: Currency Conversions

The currency conversion to USD based on the Balance sheet rate (BS) and based on the current available rate should be carried in the update rule / start routine of the ODS.

I have the following ODS defined.

AP and AR account ODS. They have chosen the following unit characteristics:

oCURKEY_LC Local currency LCURR T001-WAERS
oCURKEY_TC Document currency WAERS BSIK-WAERS

What is the correct module to use?

A: You can try using function module RSW_CURRENCY_TRANSLATION.

You can call this function module in the Start Routine of the update rules. For example:

```
Move DATA_PACKAGE-YrAmt to S_AMT_1.
CALL FUNCTION 'RSW_CURRENCY_TRANSLATION'
EXPORTING
I_CTTNM = 'YrCurrConvType'
I_AMOUNT = S_AMT_1
I_SCUR = DATA_PACKAGE-YrSrcCurr
I_TCUR = YrTrgtCurr
I_TIME_IOBJVL = CALMONTH (yrTimeRef)
IMPORTING
E_AMOUNT = ConvertedAmt
E_TCUR = YrTrgtCurr
```

Question 25: Currency exchange rate

We are currently using USD and we are going to do billing in different currencies. I understand there are several places the conversion can take place in BW and how the global settings work. Now, when the billing transactions come over to BW, do they carry the exchange rate at the time the transaction took place?

A: The transactional data will usually not carry the exchange rate, but the exchange rates are maintained in BW (and usually a job is set up to upload them from the source system). You will need to use or define currency conversion types (transaction RRC1 and RRC2) that will outline the exchange rate type, the time reference and the source and target currencies. Then you use these currency conversion types when doing the conversion in the load process or in the query.

You can look at the TCUR* tables to get a better idea of this, or run SE38 > RCURTEST.

It allows you to enter the source and target currency, rate type and time reference, and then delivers the rate. It is easier than looking up tables and helps to validate the data later on.

Question 26: Foreign Exchange (forex) transactions

What are some of the steps to configure forex fluctuations?

A: Here are some steps to configure foreign currency fluctuations:

1. Creation of 3 GL accounts.

a)IDBI Foreign Currency Term Loans under secured loans.
b)Forex profitàother income group.
c)Forex lossà Administration group.
The transaction code is FS00
Create the GL account no: 100301
Company code: NFAL
Select with template button.
Give the GL Account no: 100300
Company code : NFAL & Enter & Enter.
Select type/description tab.
Give short & long text : IDBI F C term loan.
Select control data tab.
Account currency : USD
Deselect: only balances in local currencies.
Save.

Give GL Account no: 300100
Company code: NFAL
Give the GL Account no: 400100 (salaries)
Company code: NFAL & Enter.
Give the account group: other income.
Short & Long text: Forex profit.
Save.

GL Account no: 400301
Company code: NFAL
Select with template button.
GL Account no: 400300(Rent account)
Company code: NFAL & Enter.

Give the account group: Administration.

Short& long text: Forex loss
Save.

2. Define valuation methods (OB59)

Select new entries button.
Valuation method: NFAL
Description: F C Valuation bank selling method for NFAL.
Select always valuate.
Document type: SA
Debit bal. exchange rate type: B (bank selling)
Credit bal. exchange rate type: B
Select determine rate type from account balance.
Save.

3. Prepare automatic postings for foreign currency valuation (OBA1)

Double click exchange rate difference using exchange rate key.
Give the chart of accounts NFAL
Enter.
Exchange rate difference key: USD
Expense account: 400301
Exchange rate gains account: 300100
Save.

Assign exchange rate difference key in loan master (FS00)
Give the GL Account no: 100301
Company code: NFAL
From the menu select GL Account à change.
Select control data tab.
Exchange rate difference key: USD
Save.

4. Foreign currency term loan receipt (F-02)

Give the date: current date.
Type: SA
Company code: NFAL
Currency: USD rate: 45
Posting key: 40
Account no: 200100
Enter.
Give the amount: 1000

Business area: NFAH
Text: F C term loan receipt.
Posting key: 50
Account no: 100301
Enter.

Amount:*
Business area: NFAH
Text: +
Select documentà simulate & enter.

5. Enter exchange rate on 31.3.2005 in forex table (OB08)

Select new entries button.
Exchange rate: B
Valid from: 31.3.2005
From currency: USD
To currency: INR
Direct quotation: 50
Exchange rate: G valid from: 31.3.2005
From: USD
To: INR
Save.

6. Forex run (F.05)
Give the company code: NFAL
Evaluation key date: 31.3.2005
Valuation method: NFAL
Valuation in currency type: 10 (company code currency)
Select GL balances tab.
Select valuate GL Account balances.
Give the GL Account no: 100301
Select execute button.
It will show the accounts.
Select back arrow 2 times.

Select balance sheet preparation valuation tab.
Select create postings check box.
Execute.
Message: document 27 posted in NFAL.

Go & See the document (FB03)

Document no: 27

Company code: NFAL
Fiscal year: 2004 & Enter.
Select change current layout button.
Select amount in local currency fields from hidden fields' column.
Select left arrow or show selected fields' button.
Select copy button at bottom.
Here amount 2000, it will show.

7. Post the document with out selecting line item:

Block this GL Master account for postings.
Give the GL account no. which is to be blocked.
i.e. account number 100001.
From the menu select GL Account block.
Select all the check boxes.
Save.

8. Run a program for activating line item display (SE38)
Give the program name: RFSEPA01
Execute.
Give the company code: NFAL
Give the GL Account : 100001
Select list log check box.
Execute.

Go and un block GL Master.-->FS00
Give the GL Account no: 100001
Company code: NFAL
From the menu select GL Account block.
Deselect all the check boxes
Save.

Go to the GL Account FS10N
Give GL Account no: 100001
Company code: NFAL
Fiscal year: 2004
Business area: NFAH

Double click the amount to show the line item entry for that document entry.

Question 27: Rate difference

I have defined the numbers of the accounts to which the system automatically post exchange rate difference in OBA1. Now, I get an error when I try to make payment posting for customer. E.g. rate diff accounts are incomplete for account 02 currency USD. How do I correct this?

A: Try to do the following:

OBO7 define exchange rate types
OBBs define translation ratio for ex.rates
OBO8 define ex.rate values
OBD6 define spread
Again OBO7 to define link between m, b & g exchange rate types

In OBA1, you can configure the exchange rate difference in accounts for the transaction KDF. Don't give any currency in the currency field so that it will be applicable to all currencies.

Question 28: Currency conversion issues

Let's assume currency type 20 is EUR and 30 is USD.

Data loads will come over with both 20 and 30. In the update rule, we will only execute the above FM to translate currency types of 20. The conversion will read the exchange rate tables. Based on parameters passed from FM, it will calculate an exchange rate.

When a record with 20 comes in, will it have to perform a conversion? The conversion will create a new record with the USD value and currency type 30. Will the record have both USD and EUR (20 - 10EUR, 30 - 10USD)?

A: Let's say oCURTYPE 20 is your Controlling Area currency. It is not advisable for you to store data in this format, so convert the currency of this record according to the Company Code.

Data Record in communication structure:
CO_AREA---COMP_CODE----CURTYPE---AMT---CURR
CA100-----CCODE1-------20--------100---USD

Subject this to translation in update rules:
CA100-----CCODE1-------30--------115---CAD

The second record will be written to the cube accordingly.

Question 29: Foreign currency test scripts

Can you give a sample currency test script?

A: Here is a sample script for customizing foreign currency valuation:

1. Check exchange rate types (OB07)
Go to position.
Give exchange rate type: B
Enter

The Bank is buying from you when you have exports (G type). The Bank is selling to you when you have imports & expenditure (B type). The average rate type is M type (used by MM/SD).
"G" stands for standard translation at bank buying.
"B" stands for standard conversion at bank selling.
"M" stands for standard translation at average rate.

2. Define translation ratios for currency translation (OBBS or GCRF).
Select yes for the message to continue.
Select new entries.

Exrt	from	to	valid from	ratio (from)	ratio (to)
G	USD	INR	1.12.2004	1	1
B	USD	INR	1.12.2004	1	1

Save

3. Enter exchange rates (OB08)
Select new entries button.
Give exchange rate: G
Valid from: 1.12.2004
From: USD
To: INR
Direct quotation: say 45

Give exchange rate: B
Valid from: 1.12.2004
From: USD

To: INR
Relation will come automatically 1:1
Direct quotation: say 46
Save

To enter default exchange rate type B for document type SA (OBA7)

Select position button.
Give the document type: SA
Enter.
Select document type SA, and select details button.
For exchange rate type for foreign currency documents
Enter & Save.

Posting of transaction (F-02)

Give the date: 2.12.04
Type: SA
Company code: NFAL
Currency: USD
Posting key: 40
Account: 400100 –salaries & Enter.
Give the amount: 1000(dollars)
Business area: NFAH
Text: salary payment.
Enter. it is taking rs.46 (for bank selling).
Posting key: 50
Account: 200100—cash account & Enter.
Amount:*
Business area: NFAH
Text: +
Select documentà simulate.
It will show the posting in dollars (1000).
To see INR, select display currency button.
It will show in Rs.46.
Save.

When we know the rate:
Give the date: 2.12.04
Document type: SA
Company code: NFAL
Currency: USD give the rate: 50(dollar rate)
Posting key: 40

Account: 400100   & Enter.
Ignore warning message and enter.
Give the amount: 1000 dollars.
Business area: NFAH
Text: salary payment & Enter.
It will take 50/-.
Posting key: 50
Account: 200100
Enter.
Amount: *
Business area: NFAH
Text: +
Select documentà simulate.
Save.

Open Item Management: It is used for customers, vendors and some balance sheet accounts.

Balance sheet accounts:

Provision—payments like o/s expenses.
Recovery—payments like PF, ESI and TDS
Collection and payment –sales tax
All the above accounts are used open item management accounts.

We can see the accounts in 3 ways:
 Open item—salary& wags.
 Cleared items—rent.
 All items—all three items.

Select open item management check box for the account created.
There are three scenarios: full clearance, partial clearance and residual clearance.
Provisions and payment both are equal i.e. full clearing.

Rent provision:
TC: F-02
Give the document date: 4.12.04
Document type: SA
Company code: NFAL
Currency: INR
Posting key: 40

Account: 400300 –Rent account & Enter.
Give the amount: 6666
Business area: NFAH
Text: Rent provision for document.
Posting key: 50
Account: 100500 –O/S expenses & Enter.
Amount: *
Business area: NFAH
Text: +
Select documentà simulate & Save.

To view open item management account (FBL3N):

Give the GL Account no: 100500
Company code: NFAL
Select open items radio button.
Give open at key date: today's date.
Execute.
It will show the o/s items.

1. Outgoing payment (F-07)
Give the document date: 4.12.2004
Type: SA
Company code: NFAL
Currency: INR
Account: 200100—bank /cash account.
Business area: NFAH
Amount: 6666
Text: outgoing payment.
Give the open item account: 100500
Account type: SàGL Account ledgerà it will come automatically.
Select process open items button.
It will show only 2 items like 80000, 6666
It wont show 5000(it is reserved)
Reversed document will not do the payment.
Double click on payable amount 6666
Select documentà Simulate & Save.

Go & See the O/S expenses TC is FBL3N

GL Account is 100500.
Company code: NFAL
Select cleared items & Execute.
6666 will come under cleared items.

Partial payment (bills wise outstanding) F-02:

Give the document date: 4.12.04
Document type: SA
Company code; NFAL
Reference (bill no, invoice): 1234
Posting key: 40
Account: 400300 & Enter.
Amount: 50000
Business area: NFAH
Text: Rent provision for December
Posting key: 50
Account: 100500 (o/s expenses) & Enter.
Amount: *
Business area: NFAH
Text: +
Go to documentà simulate & Save.

2. Outgoing payment partially (F-07):
Give the document date: 4.12.04
Type: SA
Company code: NFAL
Reference: 1234
Account no: 200100 (cash account)
Amount: 10000
Business area: NFAL
Text: outgoing payment.
Open item selection:-
Account: 100500—o/s exp.
Account type: S
Select process open item button.
Keep the cursor on the amount field of the line item against
which we want to adjust
(50000)
Select partial payment tab.
Now it gives payment amount column.
Double click net amount field (50000)
Double click payment amount field (10000)
Select documentà simulate.
Message; correct the marked line items.
Select page down.
Double click blue color line item.
Text: give +

Save.

Go & See the GL Account (FBL3N)

Give the GL Account No: 100500
Company code: NFAL
Select open items button.
Open at key date—Today's date.
Execute.

To see Bill wise out standings:
Select change layout button.
Select reference field from column set.
Keep the cursor on text field.
Select left arrow & Enter. Reference will come before text.
Keep the cursor on reference field. Select sub total button.
It will show 1234 bill is to be paid 40000.

3. Residual Payment (F-02)
Document date: 4.12.04
Type: SA
Company code: NFAL
Reference: 5678
Posting key: 40
Account: 400300-rent account & enter.
Amount: 100000
Business area: NFAH
Text: Rent provision for December.
Posting key: 50
Account: 100500 –O/s Exp & Enter.
Amount:*
Business area: NFAH
Text: +
Documentà simulate & Save.

Out going payment using residual payment method (F-07):

Give the document date: 4.12.2004
Document type: SA
Company code: NFAL
Reference: 5678
Give the bank data:-
Account: 200100
Amount: 20000

Business area: NFAH
Text: Outgoing payment.

Give the open item selection:
Account: 100500
Account type: S
Select process open items button.
Keep the cursor on the amount field of the line item against, which we want to
Adjust (100000).
Select residual items tab.
Double click net amount field.
Double click residual items field. It will show (80000)
Documentà simulate.
It shows message, correct the marked line item.
Select page down. Double click blue color line item.
Text: +
Save.

See the GL Account (FBL3N)

Give the GL Account No: 100500
Company code: NFAL
Select open items radio button.
Open at key date—today's date.
Execute.

It will show net payable amount 80000. It won't show 20000 & 100000.

Question 30: Automatic outgoing program error

I got this error when I running automatic outgoing payment: " Company code AS01/AS01 does not appear in proposal l (date) 2209ER; correct ". What does this mean?

A: Please check the structure of the payment program configuration. You have to define CC. Here are some steps to configure the PP:

1. All company code
    - Inter-company code pmt relation
    - The company codes that process pmts
    - Cash discount
    - Tolerance days for payment
    - The customer and vendor transaction to be processed

2. Paying company code
    - Min amt of incoming/outgoing pmts
    - Forms for pmt advice and EDI
    - Bill of exchange (written order to pay another a specific sum on a specific date sometime in the future)

3. Payment method/country
- Pmt method – check bank draft etc.

4. Payment method /company code
    - Minimum/ maximum amount
    - Whether payment abroad and foreign currency is allowed
    - Grouping options
    - Bank optimization
    - Forms of payment method

5. Bank selection
- Ranking
- Amounts
- Accounts

- Expenses/ charges
- Value date

6. House bank
- House bank should be consider 1, 2, 3,--
- Currency

Question 31: GR/IR tolerance for automatic clearing

How do I customize the tolerance for automatic clearing without the Definition of Clearing Currency (SAPF124)?

A: All you have to do is define a tolerance limit (Group) and assign to the user). This group must be assigned to the particular GL Account through its master data. In this case, you need to have accounts where clearing differences (loss or gain) will go.

Check these t Codes: OBA0, OB57 and OBXZ

IMG > FA > GLA > Business Trn > Opn Itm clrg > Clrg differences

1. Define tolerance for GL Account (This tolerance to be assigned to that GL account)
2. Assign Users to Tolerance Groups
3. Create Accounts for Clearing Differences

Question 32: Valuation methods

How are foreign currency valuation done for balance sheet and P&L accounts?

A: There are many ways for FX valuation:

1. Document FX Valuation: You can translate the postings into reporting local currency using latest exchange rate.

2. At GL Level, you can define the valuation group and carry out valuation. You can have many GL accounts in one valuation group.

3. Valuation of foreign currency Treasury deals: Normally for FX revaluation, you can use one of the methods:

-SPOT-SPOT
-FORWARD-FORWARD
-NPV (Net present value method)

SAP R/3 FICO Tcodes

GL Accounts

Question 33: GL accounts

We are trying to merge a new company with the existing company which requires the creation of a few company codes. Hence, we are extending the existing chart of accounts to the new company codes to standardize the processes. What is the best way of mapping the GL accounts?

A: Try the following method:

1. Use FS15: Send to send the GL accounts. FS16: Receive to set up the GL accounts sent in the new company. For creating only a few new accounts your best bet is to do this manually and not spend time trying to develop a process.

Using the transaction FS15, you have to be careful in the settings you have made for company code specific for the chart of account. For example, the field sort key is mandatory for company code B you have recently created. But for company code A it was optional   . Your batch would have error when it finds no value for sort key.

Make sure while using this transfer from one company code to another that setting for GL are the same.

2. The best practice is to have the same GL numbers and description across the company codes, this will help you during consolidation.

It's better to have all these g/l account on the spread sheet and then use SCAT to upload it to new company code.

Question 34: Transport GL Accounts

We have copied INT chart of accounts for our client. We have to transfer some GL Accounts only to the development client. How do we stop unwanted GL Accounts from moving to the Development Client?

A: You can copy GL accounts from one client to another. Use tcode FS15 - Send. You can select which accounts you want to copy. To receive them in the new client use tcode FS16 - Receive.

Question 35: Mass blocking of GL accounts

Is there a transaction code for mass blocking of GL account at company code level?

A: You can do a mass blocking with the following path:

SPRO->Financial Accounting->GL Accounts-Master Data->GL Account and Processing Change GL Accounts Collectively->Change Company code data.

Give the company code, GL accounts and then process it. Then you can change the layout and populate "Block for posting" field. Tick for all the GL Accounts where you want to block and save.

Question 36: Reconciliation & Alternate Reconciliation Account

What is the difference between Reconciliation Account and Alternate Reconciliation Account?

A: Reconciliation accounts connect the subsidiary accounts to main GL Accounts (for
example, customer accounts, vendor accounts and assets accounts), therefore
alternative reconciliation accounts are used to collect the information with the
main customer / vendor accounts (for example, down payment, securities deposits,
guarantee, etc.). When we create a special GL indicator and use it with alternative
reconciliation accounts for vendor and customer, it collects all the information
with main reconciliation accounts.

For example:

Vendor no. 15 abc & Company:
Balance with normal account Rs. 15000
Special GL indicator A Down Payment 10000

When we browse the vendor balance report, it shows the above mentioned amount
separately.

Question 37: Open item issue

At the time of GL master creation, we have forgotten to tick the open-item management field in the control data tab and we have posted many entries. How can we get those open-items already posted?

Where we should give link to the operating chart of accounts and the country specific chart of accounts?

A: For your first question, use program RFSEPA02. You need to copy this as a 'Z' program and invalidate the initial message you receive.

Use OB62 and map country chart of accounts. You need to give the G/L Account number of Country specific chart in "Alternate Account Number" Field of G/L Account in company code data.

Question 38: Alternative Reconciliation account

What is an Alternative Reconciliation Account? What is additional log & next date in parameters in automatic payment program? What does valuation class stands in MM-FI integration?

A: Alternative reconciliation account is a GL account which is used in advance payment for customers/Vendors configuration. We are going to assign alternate reconciliation account with the special GL indicator in the configuration step. Once we enter vendor advance with the special GL indicator A, it will move to Advance from Vendors (which is Asset Account), instead of normal sundry creditors account.

Next Payment date is used in APP for calculation of vendor which falls in the next payment run date. Example: Your APP run date is 01/10/2006 and the next payment date is 10/10/2006. Hence, if there is any payment for which the due date falls before the 10/10/2006 it will pay in this APP.

Valuation Class is used in MM-FI integration to determine the GL account. The role of valuation class is to post the value of same material to different GL accounts and vice versa.

Question 39: Automated payments

I am creating a new company code 'A'. The paying company code will be 'B' and the sending company code will be 'A'. Now, I have to configure for both manual and automated payments.

How do I configure settings for cross company payments?

How can I copy the list of "reason codes" (overpayment/underpayment) defined from the old company to the new company?

A: The following is a sample procedure to run automatic payment.

Automatic Payment program (/nF110)
Db Inventory   100
Cr Vendor   100

Db Vendor   100
Cr Cash Clearing Account   100

Db Cash Clearing Account   100
Cr Bank Account   100

1. To create a Cash clearing GL Account (Account no. 113104) in (/nFS00). Make sure you check Open Item Management and Line Item Management.

2. Go to /nF110. In the Menu:
 Environment -> Maintain Configuration, then you will see the following:
-    All company codes
-    Paying company codes
-    Payment methods in Country
-    payment methods in Company code
-    Bank Determination
-    House Banks

Don't make any changes for all the company codes, Paying company codes and Payment methods in country.

In the Payment methods in company code, give your company address in the Form View field.

Then go to House Banks:

- Give your Company Code and hit enter
- Select the company code 3000 with Currency as USD and copy it

Give your own House Bank and hit enter and then say copy all and then give your Account ID: bank account Number (9 digits) and G/L account no: (cash account 113100), then save it and you will get 1 entry copied.

Select Bank Determination and then give your company Code and then select:

- Ranking order with Pmt Type C and Currency USD, then change the House Bank from 3000 to your House bank no.
- Bank Account select 3000 C USD 3000 113101 and then copy it and give your information; vp02 C USD VP02 113104. Save.
- Available Amounts select 3000 3000 5 USD 999999 9999999 and then copy it to
  vp02 vp02 5 USD 999999 9999999 then save it.

Ignore Value date and Expense/Charges.

Next Step is to create Check Lot:
Go to /nf110
Environment -> Check information -> Number Ranges

Give your information
Paying Company code:
House Bank:
Account ID:

And then click on change icon (pencil icon)
Then click on create, give the following information
Lot Number: 001
Check Number:
To:

Short Info:
And save it.

Then go to /nse38 and give the program name RFFOUS_C.

Note:
RFFOUS_C(to remember, US-Check) is the one you complied in Payment Methods in country under the Environment -> Main Configuration then check on variant and click on change. Give your variant (VP02) and select copy from CHECK to your variant (VP02) and then click on change and give the following information:
Program run date: (blank)
Identification Feature :(blank)

Paying Company Code: VP02
House Bank: VP02
Account ID: VP02
Check lot number: 001

Printer: LP01 and check Pmt Immediately
give Number of sample printouts: 0 and then click on variant Attributes (give your own variant); then save it

Now give /nf110
Rundate: 09/21/2006
identification: vp02

In the parameter tab,
Company code Pmt method Next P/date
VP02   C 09/30/2006

Vendor: 1 to 999999

In the Additional Log tab, select check.

Due date check;
Use Payment method selection if attempt is not successful.
Line items of the payment documents in the print out/data medium tab, Program Variant RFFOUS_C VP02 and then save it. Then go to status tab and you will see parameters have been entered.

Then click on proposal, start date: check start immediately and then execute it.

Hit enter key until you get started, running and created.

Go to edit -> proposal -> Proposal List; see whether your proposal has been executed without errors.

Note: If there is error goto edit -> Proposal -> delete proposal. Not due ones are not paid.

And then go back, click on payment run and execute it with start immediately.
Hit enter until it is 2 generated and 2 completed.

Then click on Printout, execute it and then give your Job name (change the last? to 1)
In the status bar, you will see your job name to be scheduled.

Make sure the payments are done in /nfb02, giving the document number (2000000000) and make sure 2000000000 ZP (amount); 2000000001 ZP (amount).

Then go to /nsp02, to see the printouts preview.

Question 40: Vendor down payment made

I configured the down payment made for vendors. I am testing it on the end user site but I got the following error: "No special G/L account defined for acct type K sp.G/L ind. A reconciliation account 100060". What does this mean?

A: Check your entries in Transaction Code OBYR. In that, against Account Type K for SGL Ind (special GL indicator) "A" you have to maintain the vendor reconciliation account and map it to the vendor down payment account.

Also, in transaction OBYR SP GL Acc configuration Sp g/l under accounts just check if your SP g/l is assigned against Recon Acc 100060. Also see in properties tab Sp g/l indicator is act, posting keys are defined (ob41), commitment warning ticked.

Try also if you can assign a reconciliation account in vendor master data and create a link between accounts payable account and down payment account on OBYR transaction code. You need to double click on special GL indicator while linking above two ledger accounts. The accounts should be reconciliation accounts; one is current asset and one is current liability.

Question 41: Advance Payment to Vendors

How do you configure do 'Advance Payment' to 'Vendors'?

A: Here are some possible steps to make an 'Advance Payment to Vendors':

- Creation of GL Account (Advance to vendors under Current Assets Loans &Advances)
- Link between Sundry Creditors & Advance to Vendors
- Assign Payment Program to Company Code
- Advance Payment Posting
- Purchase Invoice Posting
- Transfer of Advance from Special GL Account to Normal by Clearing Special GL Account
- Clearing of Normal Account

1. Creation of GL Account (FS00)

GL Account No: 200150
Company code: NFAL
Select with template button.
Give GL Account No: 100501(Sundry Creditors)
Company Code: NFAL & Enter.
Give Account Group: Current Assets Loans & Advances
Short Text & Long Text: Advance to Vendors & SAVE.

2. Link between Sundry Creditors And Advance to Vendors (OBYR)

Double click on A or Down Payment on Current Assets.
Give chart of Accounts: NFAL & Enter.
Reconciliation Account: 100501(Sundry Creditors Raw Material)
Special GL Account: 200150(Advance to Vendors) & Save.

3. Assign Payment Program to Company Code (FBZP)

SproàFinancial Accounting-àAccounts Receivable and Accounts Payableà Business

Transactions-àOutgoing Payments-àAutomatic Outgoing Paymentsàpayment Method/Bank Selection for payment programà. Set up all company codes for payment transactions.

Select New Entries button.
Company Code: NFAL
Paying company Code: NFAL &Save.

4. Advance Payment Posting (F-48)

Document Date: 19.12.2004
Type: KZ
Company Code: NFAL
Vendor Account: 1300001
Special GL Indicator: A (Down Payment)
Bank Account: 200101
Amount: 8888
Business Area: NFAH
Text: Advance Payment & Enter.
Amount: *
Business Area: NFAH
Text: +
Select Document - Simulate & Save.

Go & See the Party Account

Give the Vendor Account: 1300001
Company Code: NFAL
Select Open Item radio button.
Select Special GL Transactions & Execute.

Question 42: Assigning material and GL to cost center

I have two materials - 100 and 200 and two materials - X and Y.

I would like to configure it as follows: When material 100 is used it should go to GL X and Cost Center 500 and when material 200 is used it should go to GL Y and Cost center 500. I need to do settings in VKOA/OBYA. Substitution is the last thing I should do. How can I do this then?

A: Go to transaction Code OBYC and then to transaction BSX. Assign different valuation class to the above materials. Then make 2 entries for each valuation class and modifier and assign the respective GL accounts.

Try also to check which valuation class is used in the material master. If same valuation class is used in the material master then change the valuation class of one material and assign a different GL account to the same in the obyc/bsx transaction. The same valuation cannot be assigned to two different GL accounts.

Question 43: Configure FICO reconciliation

How do you configure FI/CO reconciliation?

A: We create Reconciliation accounts to keep Fi GL in balance with CO. Not all transactions affect FI GLs, the best example of it is internal order settlements. They use secondary cost elements and do not affect your G/l accounts. To update the FI side of it, we maintain reconciliation accounts. These are primarily for cross company, cross functional and cross business area transactions.

The number of reconciliation accounts to be defined is dependant on various factors, like how your management wants to see the reports. Whether they want to classify the cost based on CO object class or by Co types, etc.

The basic configurations you can follow are:

1. Activate Reconciliation accounts (if you have created CO area newly, it would be active).
    Use T code: KALA

2. Assignment of Recon document type to the Controlling area.
    Use T code: OKKP

3. Creating clearing accounts.
    During FI-Co recon, inter company clearing accounts will be automatically credited or
    debited and now you need to create offset account which will show up in P&L account.
    Account determination set up thru T code: OBYA

4. Maintain accounts for Automatic Reconciliation posting.
    T code: OBYB

5. Assign Number ranges to Reconciliation activity.
    T code: OK13

Question 44: Configuration for Special Purpose Ledger

Why do we use special purpose ledger? What are the configurations that we need to make?

A: We are using the Special Purpose Ledger for statutory reporting or management reporting purpose. It also helps us in doing single entry, adjustment posting like income tax depreciation.

Steps for configuration:
-   Define Table Group
    Financial Accounting -> Special Purpose Ledger -> Basic Settings -> Tables ->
    Definition -> Define Table Group
-   Maintain Field Movement
    GCF2
    IMG Menu Path:
    Financial Accounting -> Special Purpose Ledger -> Basic Settings -> Master
    Data -> Maintain Field Movements
-   Maintain Ledger for statutory ledger
    GCL2
    IMG Menu Path:
    Financial Accounting -> Special Purpose Ledger -> Basic Settings -> Master
    Data -> Maintain Ledgers -> Copy Ledger
    Assign Co Code
    Assign Activities
-   Define Versions
    GCW1
    IMG Menu Path:
    Financial Accounting -> Special Purpose Ledger -> Periodic Processing ->
    Currency Translation -> Define Versions
-   Set Up Exchange Rate Type
    OC47
    IMG Menu Path:
    Financial Accounting -> Special Purpose Ledger (r) Periodic Processing ->

Currency Translation -> Set Up Exchange Rate Type
- Create Number ranges
    GC04
    IMG Menu Path:
    Financial Accounting -> Special Purpose Ledger -> Actual
Posting -> Number
    Ranges -> Maintain Local Number Ranges
- Create Currency Translation document type
    GCBX
    IMG Menu Path:
    Financial Accounting -> Special Purpose Ledger -> Actual
Posting -> Maintain
    Valid Document Type
- Create Posting period variant
    GCP1
    IMG Menu Path:
    Financial Accounting -> Special Purpose Ledger -> Actual
Posting -> Posting
    Period -> Maintain Local Posting Period

Question 45: Cost elements not created for GL

How can I find out the GL accounts of Profit & Loss type for which Cost Elements have not been created? Is there a standard report to throw these exceptions?

A: The first thing that comes to mind is to download the GL Accounts, download Cost Elements and do a quick VLookup in Excel.

Or, you could try these respective transactions:
OKB2:
OKB3:
SM35:

To prevent creating of GL P&L items without creating the cost elements on 4.6 / 4.7, there is an option to allow the automatic creation of Cost Elements whenever a G/L account is created in a Company Code. I.e. it does not create when an account is created at the Chart of Accounts Level, only when it is created in a Company Code.

To do this;
// Financial Accounting // General ledger Accounting // G/L Accounts // Master Records // Preparations // Edit Chart of Accounts List // Select the Chart of Accounts then; Integration // Controlling Integration // then I'll let you guess.

Also, you need to specify within controlling which account ranges should be created under which Cost Element Category; // Controlling // Cost Element Accounting // Master Data // Cost Elements // Automatic Creation of Primary and Secondary Cost Elements // *.*

If this was configured, you could also create a batch file now that would catch up with any cost elements not yet created.

Question 46: Calculate bank interest

What is the procedure to run bank interest calculation?

A: In the SAP system, defined interest calculations have two types:

1. Balance interest calculation.
2. Item interest calculation.

System defined variant for balance interest calculation type is 'S' and item interest calculation type is 'P'. Balance interest type calculation is used for G L Accounts. Item interest type calculation is used for vendors and customers.

Display of all transaction codes:
Go to t code: SE16
Table name: TSTC
Keep blank maximum number of hits.
Total transaction codes in SAP 70837.

The following steps are involved in interest calculation:

1. Define interest calculation types (OB46)
2. Prepare account balance interest calculation (OBAA)
3. Define reference interest rate (OBAC)
4. Define time dependent terms (OB81)
5. Enter interest values (OB83)
6. Creation of G L Accounts (FS00)
7. Define automatic posting (OBV2)
8. Entry for loan (F-02)
9. Interest calculation run (F.52)

1. Define interest calculation types (OB46):

Spro/img/financial accounting/G L Accounting/business transactions/bank ACCOUNT   interest calculation/interest calculation global settings/define interest calculation types

Go to new entries

Interest Id calculation type	Name	Interest
V1	balance interest type	S
V2	item interest type	P

Save

2. Prepare account balance interest calculation (OBAA):

Spro/img/financial accounting/GL Accounting/business transactions/bank account interest calculations/interest calculation global settings/prepare account balance interest calculation.

Go to new entries:
Give calculation indicator : V1
Interest calculation frequency : 01
Calendar type : G (28, 29, 30, 31)
Give number range : 03
Select balance plus interest
Save

Go to new entries:
Calculation indicator : V2
Interest calculation frequency : 01
Calendar type : G
Number range : 03
Select balance +interest
Save

3. Define reference interest rate (OBAC):

Spro/img/financial accounting/G L Accounting/business transactions/bank account interest calculation/interest calculation/define reference interest rates

Go to new entries:
Reference interest rate : V1
Long text : 12%balanace interest
Short text : 12% balance interest
Date from : 1.4.2006

Currency	: Inr
Save	

Go to new entries F8:

Reference interest rate	: V2
Long text	: 15% item interest
Short text	: 15% item interest
Date from	: 1.4.2006
Currency	: Inr
Save	

4. Define time dependent terms (OB81):

Spro/img/financial accounting/ G L Accounting/business transactions/bank account interest calculation/interest calculation/define time dependent terms

Go to new entries:

Interest calculation indicator	: V1
Currency key	: Inr
Effective from	: 1.4.2006
Sequential no	: 01
Term	: debit interest balance interest cal
Reference interest rate	: V1
Save	

Go to new entries or f8:

Interest calculation indicator	: V1
Currency	: Inr
Effective from	: 1.4.2006
Sequential no	: 02
Term	: credit interest balance interest cal
Reference interest rate	: V1
Save	

Go to new entry or f8;

Interest cal. Indicator	: V2
Currency	: Inr
Effective from	: 1.4.2006
Sequential no	: 01

Term	: debit interest
arrears interest cal	
Reference rate	: V2
Save	

Go to new entry or f8:	
Interest cal. Indicator	: V2
Currency	: Inr
Effective from	: 1.4.2005
Sequential from	: 02
Term	: credit interest
arrears interest cal	
Reference rate	: V2
Save	

5. Enter Reference Interest Rate Values (OB83):

Spro/img/financial accounting/G L Accounting/business transactions/bank ACCOUNT interest calculation/interest calculation/enter interest values

Go to new entries:

Reference int. rate values	Effective from	
Interest rate		
V1	1.4.2006	12
V2	1.4.2006	15
Save		

Go to T.Code:OBD4 to create secured loans account group.

Go to new entries:

Chart of accounts	Account group	Name	From
account to account			
1116	SELO	secured loans	100300
100399			
1116	INTR	interest	400100
400199			
Save			

6. Creation of G L Accounts (FS00):

G L ACCOUNT no	: 100305
Company code	: 1116
Select create button	
Account group	: secured loans

Select balance sheet account
Short text : I B O D Account
Long text : Indian bank overdraft
account

Select control data tab.

Select only balances in local currencies
Select open item
Select line item display
Sort key : 002

Select create/bank/interest tab

Field status group : G005
Select relevant to cash flow
Interest calculation indicator : V1
Save
Give G L ACCOUNT no : 400105
Company code : 1116
Select create button
Account group : interest
Select profit and loss account
Short text : interest on O D
Account
Long text : interest on O D
Account

Select control data tab.

Select only balances in local currencies
Select line item display
Sort key : 002

Select create/bank/interest tab
Field status group : G001
Save

7. Define automatic posting account (OBV2):

Spro/img/financial accounting/G L Accounting/business
transactions/bank ACCOUNT interest calculations/interest
posting/prepare G L ACCOUNT balance interest calculation

Go to accounts:
Chart of accounts   : 1116

ACCOUNT symbol	Currency	G
L ACCOUNT		
0002	Inr	400105
(interest on o d account)		
2000	Inr	100305 (I B o d
account)		

Save

8. Entry for loan (F-02):

Give document date   : 1.4.2006
Posting date   : 1.4.2006
Type   : SA
Company code   : 1116
Currency   : INR
Posting key   : 40
G L Account   : 200005(Indian bank account)
Enter
Amount   : 2500000
Business area   : TISC
Value date   : 16.07.2006
Text   : loan received
Posting key   : 50
G L Account   : 100305(bank of Baroda O D
account)
Enter
Amount   : *
Business area   : TISC
Text   : +
Save

9. Interest calculation run (F.52):

Accounting/financial accounting/general ledger/periodic
processing/interest calculation/balances

Give chart of accounts   : 1116
G L ACCOUNT no   : 100305 (bank
o d account)
Company code   : 1116
Calculation period   : 1.7.2006 to 31.7.2007

Select leap year
Select post also if value date in past
Select update master records
Execute

Go to system on menu bar.
Select services
Select batch input.
Select sessions.
Select RFSZIS00.
Select process.
Select display errors only
Again select process.

System gives the message: "Processing of batch input session completed";

Question 47: Special G/L transaction

What are special g/l transactions?

A: We use Special G/L transaction in down payments received and down payments made. We make a special G/L reconciliation account or down payment account in our chart of accounts. Whenever our down payment is made or received, it will not hit the A/P recon account automatically. It will hit this Special G/L account. When we clear our down payment, we move our down payment from this special G/L account to our A/P or A/R recon account.

But before doing this, we have to establish link between these two accounts in Transaction Code OBXR for customers and OBYR for Vendors. Remember to establish link in both indicators A & F.

Special GL Transactions are treated with a special reconciliation account other than the normal one. Special Gl transactions include:
  A-Down payments
  B-Bills of Exchange
  G-Guarantees
  E-Reserve for bad debts

Question 48: GL Accounts not be displayed

We have copied INT Chart of Accounts for our client. GL accounts of tax are not necessary. How do I configure so that user does not see them?

A: You can block those accounts. Blocking any G/L Accounts / Customer / Vendor accounts only restrict posting, however you can view the account. But in your case of "Not to display the G/L Accounts at end user" requires development of a G/L Account Authorization: Field name "BEGRU"

The authorization group allows extended authorization protection for particular objects. The authorization groups are freely definable. The authorization groups usually occur in authorization objects together with an activity.

Question 49: Entries in particular Field in GL

I want to see how many GL accounts were checked with Interest Indicator. How do I do this?

A: Use Transaction code SE16 to download Chart of accounts (Table name SKB1 - which is G/L account master for company code). In the selection screen, select the relevant fields including your company code and execute. The results will reflect all fields included in this table. You could use the change layout facility to include/ exclude the fields you require for review. This will surely include the "G/L account" and the "Interest Indicator" fields. Use the sort keys to identify, which G/L accounts are included against a particular Interest indicator.

Question 50: Amount transfer from bank to bank

We are in 4.6C. While executing the transaction FBZ5, the system is giving the following error: "No accts specified for company code 1000 payment method C and currency INR".

Our systems setting for automatic payment are as follows:

We have maintained one GL account for outgoing and incoming payment i.e. account end with "1" as transaction account and GL account end with "0" maintained for House bank for entered bank statement account. For example:
- House bank is BMAH1 GL account for House bank is 104200
- House bank is BMAH1 transaction account GL Account is 104201

GL accounts maintained for house bank are as under:
- House bank BMAH1: house bank GL Account is 104200 and transaction GL Account is 104201
- House bank BIAH1: house bank GL account is 104010 and transaction GL account is 104011

Setting in bank determination; FBZP are as under:
- House bank BMAH1 GL Account 104201
- House bank BIAH1 GL account 104011
- We are transferring the amount from house bank BMAH1 to House bank BIAH1

We have entered the transaction from T Code f-02. Created the cheque no. for document from T Code: FCH5 when taking the cheque print from T Code: FBZ5

System is giving following error: "No accts specified for company code 1000 payment method C and currency INR"

If we remove this house bank (from FBZP) of giving the cheque then system is taking the printout.

How do I rectify that error?

A: Check the consistency of FBZP. After going into the T-Code-->Utilities-->Error analysis, mention your Cocd and press F8.

It should not display any inconsistency your payment program has. Correct accordingly.

SAP R/3 FICO Tcodes

Chart of Accounts

Question 51: Chart of Accounts

What is a chart of account? How many charts of accounts can be assigned to a company?

A: This is a list of all G/L accounts used by one or several company codes:

For each G/L account, the chart of accounts contains the account number, account name, and the information that controls how an account functions and how a G/L account is created in a company code.

You have to assign a chart of accounts to each company code. This chart of accounts is the operating chart of accounts and is used for the daily postings in this company code.

You have the following options when using multiple company codes:

You can use the same chart of accounts for all company codes. If the company codes all have the same requirements for the chart of accounts set up, assign all of the individual company codes to the same chart of accounts. This could be the case if all company codes are in the same country.

In addition to the operating chart of accounts, you can use two additional charts of accounts. If the individual company codes need different charts of accounts, you can assign up to two charts of accounts in addition to the operating chart of accounts. This could be the case if company codes lie in multiple countries.

The use of different charts of accounts has no effect on the balance sheet and profit and loss statement. When creating the balance sheet or the profit and loss statement, you can choose whether to balance the company codes which use different charts of accounts together or separately.

Charts of accounts can have three different functions in the system:

1. Operating chart of accounts:

The operating chart of accounts contains the G/L accounts that you use for posting in your company code during daily activities. Financial Accounting and Controlling both use this chart of accounts.

You have to assign an operating chart of accounts to a company code.

2. Group chart of accounts:

The group chart of accounts contains the G/L accounts that are used by the entire corporate group. This allows the company to provide reports for the entire corporate group.

The assigning of a corporate group chart of accounts to a company code is optional.

3. Country-specific chart of accounts:

The country-specific chart of accounts contains the G/L accounts needed to meet the country's legal requirements. This allows you to provide statements for the country's legal requirements.

The assigning of a country-specific chart of accounts to a company code is optional.

The operating chart of accounts is shared by Financial Accounting as well as Controlling. The accounts in a chart of accounts can be both expense or revenue accounts in Financial Accounting and cost or revenue elements in cost/revenue accounting.

Question 52: Transport of chart of accounts

I want to transport a chart of account from one system to another. I have used OBY9, but while it works fine for the Chart of Account segment, it doesn't transport the Company Code segment. Is this possible? What transaction should I use?

A: Try the Send/Receive transactions from the user side.

Accounting > Financial Accounting > General Ledger > Master Records > G/L Accounts > Compare Company Code >

FS15 - Send
FS16 – Receive

Question 53: Copy GL account from COA

I want to copy some accounts from Chart of accounts to one of the company codes. How do I copy an account if it exists in chart of accounts but not in any of the company codes?

A: Try Tr. code OB_GLACC01:
Select all accounts which you want to copy & click on GL account. Select the account you want to copy click on Account determination.

Question 54: Transporting COA, Cost Center & Profit Center Hierarchies

My client has not set up the full Chart of Accounts, Cost Center and Profit Center hierarchies in their training client. Is there a way to copy these over from QA client without bringing a lot of transactional data with it?

A: Use T code OKE6 to transport company master data. Standard hierarchy also moves with OKE6. You have to select it under proper tab or open your standard hierarchy, go to top menu, select transport and save.

Question 55: Create and assign multiple FS to CC

How to create and attach multiple Financial Statements to my company code?

A: You have to create multiple financial statement versions for that. Create as many financial statements as you desire. You need not assign them to your company code as you create them at the chart of accounts level.

Here is the path:

Financial Accounting > General Ledger Accounting > Business Transactions >Closing > Document (ing) > Define Financial Statement Versions.

You can create multiple Financial Statements referencing one Chart of Accounts.

SAP R/3 FICO Tcodes

COPA

Question 56: COPA tables

We are using FISL and COPA with segment number as a common key. In Account COPA, I see two tables; CE4XXXX and the other is CE4XXXX_ACCT. What is the difference between these two tables? Which table should I use for reporting and reconciliation?

A: In Release 4.5A, a new table CE4xxxx_ACCT (xxxx = operating concern) is generated in addition to the existing key table CE4xxxx. This new table contains the assignment information for each document in the other applications. You may need to monitor the growth of this table.

Table CE4xxxx_ACCT contains external account assignment information as well as the characteristics for CE4xxxx and serves as the "interface" to other applications.

I recommend that you use CE4XXXX_ACCT as this is the new release table. However, if you're searching for data prior to 4.5A (probably historical data) then you might want to look into CE4XXXX if data is not found in CE4XXXX_ACCT.

Question 57: Adding Fields to COPA Data Source

I would like to add fields to COPA data source. To do this, do I have to at first delete the data source and then create new data source? In the Interface on which data source can be generated, creating and deleting are possible, but changing seems to be impossible.

A: If you are adding the fields from the same "Operating concern", go to KE24 and edit the data source and add your fields. However if you are adding fields outside the "Operating concern" then you need to append the extract structure and populate the fields in user exit using ABAP code.

Try these steps:

1) Add the fields to the operating concern. So that the required field is visible in CE1XXXX table and other concerned tables CE2XXXX, CE3XXXX etc.

2) After you have enhanced the operating concern then you are ready to add it to the CO-PA data source. Since CO-PA is a regenerating application, you can't add the field directly to the CO-PA data source. You need to delete the data source and then need to re-create using   KEB2 transaction.

3) While re-creating the data source, use the same old name so that there won't be any changes in the BW side when you need to assign the data source to info-source. Just replicate the new data source in BW side and map the new field in info-source. If you re-create using a different name, then you need extra build efforts to take the data into BW through IS all the way top to IC. I suggest that you keep the same old data source name as before.

Question 58: COPA Extraction

We have created a COPA data source using KEB0. When we execute the same in RSA3, we get @ 16 records whereas there are around 1500 records which can be seen in KE24 (Display Actual Line Items) transaction in R/3.

For the above 16 records, the characteristic values are not getting populated, we could see only the Key figures. What are we missing?

A: COPA data sources behave this way in RSA3 especially with a large number of characteristics and value fields as part of its extraction.

What you get in BW is perfect. Follow the how to document and that's all is needed.

Again, in RSA3, COPA data sources show funny stuff and don't show the actual records.

To validate what the DS has extracted into BW, go to CE1XXXX table in R/3 and do a record to record comparison with the cube. Although your CE1XXXX table would have thousands of records and your cube has only 1500 records (due to aggregation), do check at a company code level or some other field level in the table. In CE1XXXX, the XXXX is the operating concern's name.

Question 59: Extraction steps

What are some possible COPA extraction steps? Why is COPA different from other extraction (e.g. LIS/LO etc.) mechanisms?

A: COPA Extraction steps:

R/3 System:
1. KEB0
2. Select Datasource 1_CO_PA_CCA
3. Select Field Name for Partitioning (E.g., Ccode)
4. Initialize
5. Select characteristics & Value Fields & Key Figures
6. Select Development Class/Local Object
7. Workbench Request
8. Edit your Data Source to Select/Hide Fields
9. Extract Checker at RSA3 & Extract

BW:
1. Replicate Data Source
2. Assign Info Source
3. Transfer all Data Source elements to Info Source
4. Activate Info Source
5. Create Cube on Infoprovider (Copy str from Infosource)
6. Go to Dimensions and create dimensions, Define & Assign
7. Check & Activate
8. Create Update Rules
9. Insert/Modify KF and write routines (const, formula, abap)
10. Activate
11. Create InfoPackage for Initialization
12. Maintain Infopackage
13. Under Update Tab Select Initialize delta on Infopackage
14. Schedule/Monitor
15. Create Another InfoPackage for Delta
16. Check on DELTA OptionPls r
17. Ready for Delta Load

LIS, CO/PA, and FI/SL are Customer Generated Generic Extractors, and LO is BW Content Extractors.

LIS is a cross application component LIS of SAP R/3, which includes, Sales Information System, Purchasing Information System, Inventory Controlling.

Similarly CO/PA and FI/SL are used for specific Application Component of SAP R/3.

CO/PA collects all the OLTP data for calculating contribution margins (sales, cost of sales, overhead costs).

FI/SL collects all the OLTP data for financial accounting, special ledger;

Difference: CO-PA / LIS / LO / FI-SL

1) Method for Delta: Time Stamp / LIS Info Structure / Change Log / Pseudo Delta

2) Application Specific: All are

3) Extractors: Customer Generated (CG) / SAP BW Content / CG / CG

4) Tables Used: Line item tables / 1 structure (s5nn). 2 tables (BWl1 and 2) and control change log (TMCBIW) / V3 update (asynchronous) and two tables: VBDATA and ARCFC (change log from SAP R-3 / Three types of tables - Line Item Tables- ZZP (plan) & ZZA (actual), - Total Table ZZT, - Objects Tables ZZO & ZZC

Also, the Logistics extraction and other extractions like FI, and COPA have a different extraction technology.

In LO extraction, the setup reads the dataset that you want to process such as, customer orders with the application tables VBAK, VBAP and fill the relevant communication structures with data. The data is stored in cluster tables from where it is read when the initialization   is   run.

Other extractions like FI, CO-PA works based on timestamp criteria, so every delta will take records changed or modified after the timestamp of the last loaded record (even if there is a safety interval).

One of the main differences is that the CO/FI data sources are "pull based", meaning that the delta mechanism is based on a time stamp in the source table and data is pulled from these tables into the RSA7 queue. The LIS data sources are "push" based meaning, that the delta mechanism is based on an intermediary queue to which the delta records are pushed on time of transaction. From the intermediary the delta records are transferred to RSA7 queue. This is done by an R/3 scheduled job independent of BW extractions.

Question 60: COPA does not reconcile between BW and R/3

We have recently started a project in BW to load COPA (cost based accounting) data for 2005-2006. Starting on 07/21/2006, after R/3 summarization level jobs were completed and up to date, I ran FULL loads by fiscal period starting with 01/2005 and ending with 07/2006. The loads completed on 07/25/2006. During this time, no further summarizations were done in R/3. I then ran an "Initialization without data transfer" in BW with no selection criteria. Starting with the following day, 07/26/2006, deltas were run on a mostly daily basis.

On 08/06/2006, a delta failed because of an invalid character "°" in one of the characteristics. The record count for this failed load was 1,233,125.

I then set the status to red, and deleted the request from the cube. I then wrote update rules to fix the bad data coming from R/3 ("DE°2" changed to "DE02"). On 08/08/2006 a repeat of the delta was run successfully and the record count matched the previous failure (1,233,125).

During the time the delta loads started on 07/26, the finance team has been making constant adjustments to 2006 (all periods) data. On 08/10/2006, it was found that for a given material #, COPA and BW were not in agreement. We are not sure if it is related to the 08/06/2006 delta failure or something else. All other delta loads from this source have been successful except for the one on the 6th.

What steps can I take to avoid missing data? How can I make sure that deltas are properly capturing all the data?

A: To check the records:

1) Go to KEB2 and compare the time stamps for your last delta extractions. You can also see the number of records read and sent to the BW system. To be sure, follow the next step.

2) Go to CE1XXXX (XXXX - Operating Concern) table and with

the delta selections and time stamp range from KEB2, see if there was any posting happened during that time period or not.

Compare the number entries in the table with the number of records 'Read' from KEB2. If both matches, then you can be very sure that nothing was missed in your delta.

Question 61: Index use

How do you check if an 'Index' is being used?

A: Sometimes a suitable index is not used for a selection, even if one exists. Which index is used depends on which optimizer the database system uses. To check whether an index is being used, proceed as follows:

1. Open a second session and choose System > Utilities > Performance Trace there.
2. Select SQL Trace and choose 'Trace on'.
3. In the first window, carry out the action for which you want the system to use the desired index.
4. Choose 'Trace off' and then trace list.
5. The display generated depends on the database system used. You can find the index used with the function EXPLAIN on the critical statements (PREPARE, OPEN, REOPEN).

If your database system uses a cost-based optimizer, you should carry out step 3 with as representative a data volume as possible, since a cost-based optimizer finds the best index on the basis of statistics.

Question 62: Improve I/O

Is there a simple way to improve I/O?

A: In standard installations, the system can typically read about 200,000 records per hour from the segment level. This performance is largely independent of the hardware used. However, if you have four table spaces available (for example, PSAPCE4D, PSAPCE4I, PSAPCE3D and PSAPCE3I) which are stored on four different hard drives, you can distribute the data in CO-PA as follows:

- Table CE4xxxx in table space PSAPCE4D
- Indexes CE4xxxxn for table CE4xxxx in table space PSAPCE4I
- Table CE3xxxx in table space PSAPCE3D
- Primary index CE3xxxxo for table CE34xxxx in table space PSAPCE3I

If no data has been posted to Profitability Analysis in your system yet, it makes sense to redefine the parameters for those database objects using the database utility (transaction SE14). Otherwise you will have to back up the existing data before the conversion and then restore it later, a time-consuming process.

This solution which can be achieved with relatively little effort can usually increase the typical speed at which the system reads the segment level to about 500,000 records per hour.

Question 63: COPA delta

How do I reformat delta for the COPA Cube? The cube has no data. But when I try to into the info package it fives me an abap dump, some message RSM 000. The description in that message: The current application program detected a situation which really should not occur. Therefore, a termination with a short dump was triggered on purpose by the key word MESSAGE (type X).

In Error Analysis it displays:

Short text of error message:
*** Data request to the OLTP ***

Technical information about the message:
Message class...... "RSM"
Number.............. 000
Variable 1.......... " "
Variable 2.......... " "
Variable 3.......... " "
Variable 4.......... " "
Variable 3.......... " "
Variable 4.......... " "

And in trigger location it displays:

Program SAPLRSS1
Include LRSS1F11
Row 1,365
Module type (FORM)
Module Name RSM1_CHECK_FOR_DELTAUPD

A: You need to clean up the Delta indicator. You can do this by deleting entries from the table. Here are the steps:

Reference OSS note: 852443

1. Check RSA7 on your R3 to see if there is any delta queue for COPA.
2. On BW go to SE16 and open the table RSSDLINIT
3. Find the line(s) corresponding to the problem data source.

4. You can check the load status in RSRQ using the RNR from the table

5. Delete the line(s) in question from RSSDLINIT table

6. Now you will be able to open the info package. So now you can ReInit.

7. In the info package go to the 'Scheduler' menu > 'Initialization options for the source system' and delete the existing INIT (if one is listed).

Question 64: Billing issue

Sales order is created with Billing Plan. Billing is sales order related and not with reference to the delivery. The delivery is created with reference to the sales order.

The billing plan has multiple Billing stages and the final billing stage is done after sales order is completely delivered and PGI. The billing documents until the last billing document is posted to Accrual Account and when the final billing is done, in the pricing procedure we have 4 condition types, which adds up all the accruals (Net Amount) in the previous billing documents and Material Account Documents and post to actual, whereas the final billing amount is posted to actual.

The system is so configured that it doesn't generates COPA document for the accruals, i.e. for all the billing documents before the final billing. Sales Quantity, Cost of Goods Sold and Revenue are posted to COPA when final billing is done.

Revenue and Cost of goods sold is updated as required whereas sales quantity is not updated in COPA. Please note, if we activate COPA for accruals, then the quantity is updated in COPA for the first billing document but not for the subsequent billing documents. How can this problem be solved?

A: Make sure that the quantity fields are assigned in KE4M. Also check the conditions and see if QTY is correct in the billing line item. Next, if the QTY is not correct coming from sales then user exits in VOFM can fix this. If the quantity are correct include ZXKKEU03 in PA can be used to fix those issues.

Also, try to debug the standard program and solved the issue by include ZXVVFU08.

Question 65: Delete init request in COPA

When I try to initialize delta in COPA, I get the info:

"Delete init. Request Requ_**** before running again init with same selection"

How do I delete the request in COPA?

A: Go to info package. Menu scheduler -> Init options for source system. Delete entry corresponding to previous delta init.

Question 66: COPA extraction delta failure

The following delta extraction failed:
"1_CO_PA_010_MC01 due to lock in source system"

We repeated delta to restore this issue. However it brought 0 records in BW.

We checked RSA7 in R/3 it also displays 0 records. However in R/3 RSA3 if we try to check extraction for corresponding delta it throws error saying "error in extraction".
System also throws error saying:
"error_passed_to_mesh_handler"

How can I resolve this issue?

A: First check whether you have any records to extract or not in R/3 side. In order to check the records:

1. Go to KEB2 and compare the time stamps for your last delta extractions. You can also see the number of records read and sent to the BW system. But to make sure, follow step 2.

2. Go to CE1XXXX (XXXX - Operating Concern) table and with the delta selections and time stamp range from KEB2, see if there was any posting for that period or not. If there was no posting then it is obvious that no records will be extracted.

3. But if there were any postings and it was still not extracted, then you are in a critical situation. If you are with PI2004, then i doubt if you can still use KEB5 in this case to set the correct delta timestamp. However with PI2002, KEB5 works fine. But be careful when you set the time-stamp, otherwise you will end of with the extracting the same record twice.

Question 67: Data extraction for COPA pulling o records

On scheduling the COPA delta load, it is pulling in o Records in BW. But the consumer says that it should be pulling records.

I checked RSA7; it also shows o records. I also tried replicating the data source and re-scheduling but still pulled o records.

The data load also failed once with the error "The selected source of data is locked by another process".

Since we don't have any V3 concept here, can you let me know what exactly pulls the COPA data in RSA7?

A: RSA7 gets filled by the extractor for CO-PA extraction. Its not you post something and that gets into the delta cube. It's actually getting filled by the extractor program when the BW request was sent for extraction. So if you have 'o' records getting extracted in BW then RSA7 will also show o records only.

If your customer is saying there must be some records, then the best way is to check the CE1XXXX (XXXX - Operating concern) table. Get the time-stamp information from the table TKEBWTSN and apply those time-stamp interval in your table along with all other selection criteria that you might be using in your delta update. Check if you are getting any records or not. If you have any records and it was not extracted in BW then it's definitely a problem. Then you need to take a close look at the time-stamps and whether there were any changes to time-zone, etc.

Question 68: Increase/Decrease credit limit

How can you reverse a document posted in a previous closed period? Where can I uncheck/check a credit block on a customer?

A: If you are asking about credit management, it's done at T code fd32. There you can increase/decrease customers credit limit.

If you want see the list of blocked documents and release it, you can do it at tcode VKM1.

Question 69: A/R - Credit Management for customers

Is there a place on AR side where a user can put some credit control notes for a customer, like ticklers in case of deduction management component configuration? How can we use the ticklers for both these purposes?

A: You can add notes on either the item or customer.

In XD02, select Extras > Text

Or in FBL5N you can add text Extras > Text

Question 70: Update Customer Credit Management

How can you locate a BAPI or RFC that allows updating credit management data for a customer - more specific the "Payment index" field DBPAY (KNKK)? This is achievable through FD32 but can not find an RFC/BAPI that does the job.

A: Try fm CREDITLIMIT_CHANGE.

Question 71: Mass update customer credit limit

I need to do a mass update of the credit limit to 1 for a credit control area. I tried to do it through customer mass maintenance but the field credit limit is not allowed to be selected. Is there any program for doing so?

A: Create Transaction recording for FD32 through the transaction SHDB. Then prepare the entire list according to the fields required to be filled up exactly same as the recording.

Then go to transaction LSMW. Provide the path for the file to be uploaded. Then follow the steps to upload the file in one shot.

Question 72: Customer report with dr. balance only

Where can you find the following reports?

1. Any report that display customers with Dr. Balance (Receivables).
2. Credit Sale report.

A: To see the Dr Balance Report, you can use the T-Code S_ALR_87012169. Here you can see all the customers balance including credit balances period wise. There you can click on overview icon then click on customer. This will give you report of all customer balances. Now you can filter only on debit balances by giving condition > 0.00.

You can also try S_ALR_87012172. Report is providing the Account Balance as input, here you can give >0 which will give you only those customer who is having Dr. Balance.

Question 73: Customer credit management change BO Required

We are having a requirement of identifying the Standard Business Object for Customer Credit Management Change (FD32 Txn).

We tried finding the required BO using EVENT TRACEm but were unsuccessful.

Can anyone tell me if there is a BO attached to FD32?

A: Try to do the following:
- First go to SE93.
- Type in FD32 and display it to find out the package assigned to the transaction.
- This is FICR, double click that one and on the next screen click on display object list (CTRL+CHIFT+F5).
- Unfortunately, for this package only transactions exist.

So, click back to check what program is assigned to the transaction. This is SAPMF02C.
Double-click on the program name, and then go to attributes.
Double click package FBD and display object list again.

Now you'll see among other things Business Engineering, open that one, and then open business object types. There you'll see the following:
BUS1010
BUS3007
KNA1
KNB1
T024B
T024P

One of these probably will do the job.

Question 74: Credit Block

Is there any standard report which gives the following details in customer credit management area?

1. Customer code
2. Amount for which credit block was opened
3. Sales order no for which credit block was opened
4. User id from which credit block was opened
5. Date on which block was opened
6. Number of times the block was opened for a customer

A: Try T code VKM1, it has the most of what you are looking for.

SAP R/3 SD Transaction Codes: SD Fundamentals

Question 01: SAP Sales and Distribution Processing Document Flow

How does the document flow in SAP Sales?

A: The sales documents you create are individual documents but they can also form part of a chain of inter-related documents. For example, you may record a customer's telephone inquiry in the system. The customer next requests a quotation which you then create by referring to the inquiry. The customer later places an order on the basis of the quotation and you create a sales order with reference to the quotation. You ship the goods and bill the customer. After delivery of the goods, the customer claims credit for some damaged goods and you create a free-of-charge delivery with reference to the sales order. The entire chain of documents – the inquiry, the quotation, the sales order, the delivery, the invoice, and the subsequent delivery free of charge – creates a document flow or history. The flow of data from one document into another reduces manual activity and makes problem resolution easier. Inquiry and quotation management in the Sales Information System help you to plan and control your sales.

The following graphic shows how the various types of sales documents are inter-related and how data subsequently flows into shipping and billing documents.

Question 02: Sales Document Type

What is the different document types used for Sales?

A: Sales document can have many different document types.
Each document type has its own usage.
Some commonly used document types are:-
* OR - Standard Order
* RE - Returns
* FD - Delivery Free of Charge

Different Sales Document types have different control parameters.

For e.g. Document type ZOWN :-

General control:

Check Division

Blank -> no checks

   1 -> Dialog to inform user that the division is different from material master

   2 -> Error when division is different from material master

Shipping

Immediate Delivery

Blank -> Create delivery separately

   1 -> Create delivery immediately when sales order is save

   2 -> Create delivery if quantity can be confirmed to day

Maintain Sales Document Type
* Transaction VOV8 - Double click on the document type to check the configuration.

Some configurations you can specify:-
* Check credit limit
* Define the default Delivery type
* Define the default Billing type
* Block the Document Type from being used etc.

Question 03: New Division/Sales Area/Sales Office

What are the various tcodes for SAP SD 4.6?

A: Below is a list of references for SD 4.6x tcodes.

OVXA - Assign division to sales organization

OVXG - Set up sales area

OVXM - Assign sales office to sales area

e.g. Sales Organization -> Distribution Channel -> Division

             |

             -> Sales Office

VOR2 - Define Common Divisions

OVAN - Combine divisions allows you to share sales document type data between different divisions. You define the sales document types in a central division and then use it as a reference division.

For e.g.

Sales Organization	Division	Reference division
ALL	01	01
ALL	02	01
ALL	03	01

OVKK - Define Pricing Procedure Determination

For e.g.

Sales Organization	Distribution Channel	Division
Document Procedure	Pricing Procedure	
ALL	01	01

A   1

SM30 Table/View:

V_TSPA - Define New Division

V_T134G_WS - Assign Business Area To Plant

V_TVTA_GRE - Define Rules By Sales Area

V_TVTA_KFV - Assign business area by sales area

V_TVAKZ - Assign sales order types permitted for sales areas

Question 04: Difference between sales organization and sales area

What is the difference between sales organization and sales area?

A: Organizational Structure broadly refers to the way a company follows a set path of systems/hierarchies. Different companies do have different structures and the differences in structures emanates basically from the strategies.
Sales organization is the organizational unit which responsible for the selling of the product, movement of goods to the customer.
Sales Area is the combination of the Sales:
Organization + Distribution Channel + Division.
Company code of an organization is the legal entity which have separate Balance sheet and profit & loss ACCOUNT required by law for the legal purpose so whenever an organizational unit have different Balance sheet and P/L Account you can define a company
code.
A Company's structure can be mapped in R/3 which would facilitate flow of information, flow of process and also facilitates work flow in a logical way.
A Sales organization structure is based on the Elements of the Organization which are as follows.
1. Company Code
2. Sales Organization
3. Distribution Channel
4. Division
5. Plant
6. Shipping Point.
A Company Code is generally created by finance and it broadly represents the highest point of structure.
The relationship between Sales Org and Company code is Unique. One Sales Organization can be assigned to one Company code. Think of one practical situation where in u can Say that Essar is One Group (Client).
Essar Infotech (Company Code), Essar Oil (Company Code).
Essar Oil may have Essar South (Sales Org) and Essar North(Sales Org). You have to remember that Essar South is only assigned to Essar Oil and not Essar Infotech right....

A Combination of Sales Organizayttion, Distribution Channel and Division is called a Sales Area and a Sales Area is assigned to the company thru the Sales Orgn.
A plant is assigned to the company code. It is also assigned to the Sales Org and Dist Channel and this channel is called Delivering Plant.
A Shipping Point is assigned to the CLIENT.

Question 05: Block Sales Document Type / Delivery / Billing by Customer

When you block new orders for a specific customer?
How do you accomplish this effectively?

A: When there is a temporary stop of business with a customer, you can block new orders to be created for this customer. You can have the options of blocking all the work flow or let the delivery and billing to continue for any open orders.

VD05 - Block/Unblock Customer

OVAS - Sales Order Type Blocking reasons

OVAL - Blocking reasons links with Sales Order Type

OVZ7 - Delivery Blocking reasons

OVV3 - Billing Blocking reasons

In 4.6x, if you found that your Sales Order Billing Block is not working, it is because you need to build the Billing Block for the Billing Type.

SM30 - Table/View **V_TVFSP**

If you want a material to be blocked, go to the Basic data 1 view of the material, there in the general data you have " X-plant material status ". Also in Cost estimate 1 view of the material you have Plant Specific Material status. Use the options available to block the material in these two views.

You cannot use the material in sales order

Use the material exclusion function:

FUNCTIONALITY:

SD> Master data > Products > Listing/Exclusion> Create

(Transaction codes VBO1, VBO2, VBO3)

Enter the list/exclusion type B001: For the required

Customer:

Enter Maintain materials > Save > Exit

Create the order and enter material excluded to test exclusion.

CONFIGURATION: IMG SETTINGS

For IMG settings; Go to IMG > SD > Basic

Functions>Listing/Exclusion

Ensure that the listing/exclusion procedure is activated for your order type. You can also create your own condition types access sequences and procedures or use the SAP provided ones.

Question 06: Wrong/duplicate RE Created

How do you correct a wrong or duplicate RE?

A: These are the steps to correct the procedure:
- Check Document Flow for RE
  Decision:
    - No Goods Issue and No Credit Memo created
    - Reject the sales order item
    - No Goods Issue and Credit Memo created
      - Cancel Credit Memo
      - Reject the sales order item
    - Goods Issue and Credit Memo created
    - Create another OR to offset the credit memo created. Treat this as a normal OR process. Ensure that account receivable is informed by typing in the item text. Please do not send invoice to customer as the RE is wrongly/duplicate.

  Note: When you create another OR, the delivery department may actually go and deliver the goods to customer. Thus, it is important to inform them that this OR is for internal adjustment. The process of posting the goods issue must be done by the delivery side for proper flow.

Question 07: Movement type determination and Availability

What are the transaction codes for movement type and availability?

A: Below is a rundown of the appropriate tocdes for movement type and availability:

SM30 - Table View - **V_TVEPZ** -> Assign schedule line categories
  - First check the Proposed schedule line category (SchLC) - double click on the line item

VOV6 - Maintain the schedule line categories - double click on the line item
  - For example, you can control the default returns movement type.
  - 651 - two steps - with a transfer posting using 453
  - 653 - one steps - direct post to unrestricted used

Control the Transaction Flow (tick to activate the function)
  - transfer of requirement
  - for availability check for sales
  - production allocation active

Question 08: Sales reservation

What is the tcode setup for sales reservation usage?

A: Sales reservation takes place automatically through availability check.
The setting is on the checking group (OVZ2 - Define Checking Groups).
You must set the "Accumul." column. Without setting this it will only check availability but not reserve it!
SAP recommends Accumul. = 3 -> Accumulate the requirements quantity when creating and accumulate the confirmed quantity when making changes.
For manual reservation, you can use MB21, movement type 251 - Goods Issue for sales.

To activate the Sales Order number field, do the following:

Activate transaction OMBW;
double click movement type 251;
double click additional account assignment.
Tick the required/optional button as per your requirement.
The user has to manage the manual reservation using MBVR.
Reserving material without sales order:
In Order to reserve the specific materials for a particular customer, use Strategy 50 to plan your MRP with the materials getting reserved for customer when you make Individual / Collective requirement (1) in MRP4 view of Material Master.
Or you can create a manual reservation against that particular material and give the customer name in the Recipient Field so that you can easily identify the Material which belongs to the Customer.

Question 09: Sales Order Stock

How do you properly place the sales order stock?

A: Sales Order Stock is stock with Special Stock type E. It can fall into the usual stock categories such as unrestricted, blocked etc. but "belongs" to a sales order. For example, you create a sales order for a part and assign a sales item category that generates an individual requisition, the requirement has an account assignment linking it to the sales order schedule line, and you convert that requisition to a Purchase Order.
When you receive the Purchase Order, the stock is placed in sales order stock. It will show against the sales order/sales order line. It can only be delivered against that sales order line. Any availability check etc for that material on any other sales order will not take it into account as it is not available except to the sales order line the stock is assigned to.

Question 10: Forecasted and Confirmed Sales Orders

What is the tcode for forecasted and confirmed sales orders?

A: The tcode to use for forecasted and confirmed sales orders is MD73 – this will do a 'Display Total Requirements' functionality. Afterwards, enter the material or MRP controller you want to analyze.

Assignment field options:

1. If you with to look at how the planned independent requirements have been match to the sales order. Sales order which are over and above that forecasted are not shown.
2. If you are interested primarily in seeing what sales order are over and above the sales forecast.
3. If you are interested in seeing all the sales order with indication of whether or not they have been anticipated in the forecast.
4. If you wish to see all the three reports of the above three options together. Leave blank if you want to see a complete list of sales order, without any indication of whether they have been anticipated in the forecast.

Question 11: Backorder Processing

What is the tcode for backorder processing?

A: Backorder processing is a piece of functionality in SAP where you can change the commitments and over-ride the blockage of stock marked against sales documents/deliveries. For example, you receive an order from a very important customer for material "A" but
the entire quantity of A is committed to another customer "B" via earlier sales orders and this is where BACKORDER processing helps you to change the commitment and shift stock due for B to A. This is the benefit of this functionality.

OMIH - Checking rule for updating backorders
OPJL - Define new checking rule
OPJJ - Define scope of check
V_RA - Backorder Processing

Data selection:

Sold-to-party	Customer code	Mandatory
Sales Organization		Mandatory
Distribution Channel		Mandatory
Division		Mandatory

Changed confirmed quantity:

Tick the material you want to change and click the Backorder button
Confirmed quantity that still can be changed are highlighted.

V.15 - Backorder List

Sales Organization	Mandatory
Distribution Channel	Mandatory
Division	Mandatory

Question 12: Third Party Order Processing

How do you process third party order processing?

A: Third party order processing is done as follows:

Assume three companies X, Y and Z;

X - The company;
y - The customer;
Z – Vendor;

When ever X gets a PO from Y to supply some goods; X has an option of either manufacturing those goods or procuring those goods.
If he is procuring the goods, there are two methods that are generally followed:

Method 1) After receiving the PO from Y, X creates a sales order against Y.
Now at the same time he also creates a PO to a vendor Z to produce the goods
Z produces the goods and supplies to X
X receives the goods from Z
Then X delivers the same goods to Y.
After that X invoices Y and Z invoices X.

Note : Here there is no direct/ indirect relation between Z and Y.

This process is known as Trading Process. And the Material here is created with Material type HAWA.

The other method is a Third party order processing method:

Here the glaring difference is that instead of Z supplying the material to X and X in turn supplying the same material to Y.

X authorizes Z to supply the material to Y on his behalf and notify him once the delivery is complete.

Now Z supplies the material to Y and acknowledges the same to X.

Z will send a copy of delivery acknowledgement and invoice to X.

After receiving the delivery confirmation and invoice from Z, X has to verify the invoice and this process is known as invoice verification and is done in SAP through Transaction code MIRO.

The next step for X is to create an invoice and submit to Y. Only after the invoice verification document is posted then only X can create an invoice for Y. This is the business flow that is followed for third party order configuration. There are few steps that have to be configured to enable the system to function as mentioned above.

1. If you are always following a third party process for a material then you have to create the material using item category group BANS.

The procurement type should be marked as 'External procurement' (F) in MRP 2 view of the material master record.

If you are not always allowing third party order processing then u can create a material master record with item category group as NORM and the procurement type should be marked as (X) meaning both types of procurement (in house manufacturing and external procurement).

2. The item category in the order should be manually changed as TAS. For that you need to configure the item category determination

ord type + item cat grp + usage + Hiv level = Item cat + Manual item cat

OR + NORM +   +   = TAN . + TAS
OR + BANS +   +   = TAS

3. Make sure that during the item category configuration for TAS you need to mark relevant for billing indicator as F

4. The schedule line category for this type should be CS. Make

sure that you mark subsequent type as NB - purchase requisition in this schedule line category as this will trigger the purchase requisition order immediately after the creation of the sales order and the PO to vendor is created against this purchase requisition.

Question 13: Product Group and Sales BOM

How do you classify bulk orders and how do the sales BOM handle this?

My client collects products with quantities in something they call Product Group. The customer calls in and orders for the product group and automatically gets in all the associated materials.

Do we need a Sales Order BOM to handle this?

A: This is a good example of a Sales Order BOM. But the configuration of Sales BOM depends upon certain conditions like:
If you want to create the product group and price it at header level or if you want to assemble the products and depending upon the assemblies you want to price.
For example, if the customer asks for a certain combination of Material A, B and C respectively,
then you create a Material Master record Material D with item category group as LUMF.
While the Materials A, B and C are created with standard item category groups NORM only.
Then create a sales BOM using Transaction code CS01 and enter the following details:
Material: Material D
Plant: Plant in which you created the material.
BOM Usage: 5 (Sales and Distribution)
Then give the Materials A, B, and C and give their respective quantities before you have to create pricing condition records for Materials A, B, and C.
Then configure the item categories (T - code: VOV4).
When processing the sales order, just give the Material D and the system will pick up the corresponding assemblies for that material and populate in the order.
The item category for the header item will be TAP
and the item category for the items will be TAN,
In this case the Material D is called as the higher level Item, and all the assemblies are called as the sub items.

Here the sub items are relevant for pricing and delivery where as the header item is not relevant for neither pricing nor delivery. It just acts as a text item.

This type of configuration of BOM is known as pricing at item level. This is used when you don't know what quantities of assemblies the customer is going to order and if the price of the assembly keeps varies.
There is another way of configuring BOM which is pricing at header level.
The difference is that the Material Master D has to be configured using the item category group ERLA.
Creation of BOM is same.
But you need to maintain the pricing condition record for the header item.
The item categories in this case would be
Header item: TAQ
Sub item TAE;
Where the header item is relevant for pricing and delivery and sub items are not relevant for neither the pricing nor the delivery.
Depending upon your requirements you can configure accordingly.

Question 14: Defining Company and Assigning Sales Organization

What is the definition of a company code and how are sales assigned as per company code?

A: To determine the definition of 'Company Code', you could undertake the following steps:
1. Transaction Code: SPRO
2. Click Enterprise IMG button
3. Select Enterprise Structure -> Definition -> Financial Accounting -> Define, Copy, Delete, Check Company Code -> Edit Company Code Data
4. Check the check box and all yes radio buttons. Click Continue button
5. Click New Entries Button and Type your company code and name.
Assignment of Sales Organization to Company Code:
1. Transaction Code: SPRO
2. Click Enterprise IMG button
3. Select Enterprise Structure -> Assignment -> Sales and Distribution -> Assign Sales Organization to Company Code
The sales organization is an organizational unit within logistics, which structures the company according to its sales requirements. It represents the selling unit as a legal entity. It is responsible for product guarantees and other rights to recourse, for example. Regional subdividing of the market can also be carried out with the help of sales organizations.
Each business transaction is processed within a sales organization.
Each sales organization is assigned exactly one company code for which you enter all accounting details of the sales organization.
A distribution chain can be active for several plants and the plants can be assigned to different company codes. If the sales organization and plant are assigned to different company codes, an internal billing document is sent between the company codes before the sales transactions are entered for accounting purposes.

Question 15: Partner Procedures

What is the process of determining appropriate procedures? Can you include some definition of terms relevant to the process as well?

A: Below are samples you can go over to show partner procedures determination.
Sold-to-party (Customer Master) - Payment, Tax determination procedures:

Bill-to-party - Address to send the invoice to
Ship-to-party - Deliver the goods to
Payer - Pay to who (a company/person name)
VOPA - Maintain Partner Determination
Click Partner Object;
Click Partner Procedures;
Double Click on the Procedures Line Items to pass the partner function contact person (CP) data to the ship-to-party in the delivery document.
Go to the Partner Determination procedure for you sales order type. Look for the column that is labeled SOURCE. Put SH against partner function CP and it will assign CP from ship-to-party to afterwards.
As long as you have CP in your delivery document, it will be copied from SO to Delivery properly
One Time Customer
V-07 - Create a one-time customer. (Account Group - CPDA)
In order for the user to create sales order, you have to maintain the Account group for the Sold-to Party (SP):

VOPA - Maintain Partner Determination
Click Partner functions;
Click Environment -> Account Group Assignment;
To create a new entry, press Page Down till the last line.

Question 16: Goods Return from Customer

We have posted GI to ship the material from our plant to our customer plant in Japan (also belongs to our own company, we're doing intercom transfer). Now they want to return the material to us.
What is the process for us to do goods Return? What are the exact steps/transactions used to handle this process.
What if the billing document has been created and they have made payment to us?
What if the billing document has been created and sent but they have made payment to us?

A: All returns against sales order are affected against sales order type RE.
You can copy this order type and rename it to suit your purpose.
Kindly understand that sales returns are against billing raised.
This means while creating the sales return order, that it will be created with reference to the Billing Number. This will ensure all the original effects in the billing to be passed on to the SRA. The credit memo is based on the order and not on the delivery.
Try this first in the development server before doing it in the production server. Also, ensure to verify that the credit memo actually credits the customer and debits sales account. We had this problem due to some hot patch application in version 4.0B and then had to get the relevant code from SAP OSS for applying in the copy control routines. As regards the payment, the amount will appear as credit balance in the customer account and you need to decide whether to adjust against some other invoice or refund the amount to the party.
You won't be able to use the standard customer return process for these cases. A customer return will only do the postings on one side (goods receipt, customer credit memo), but will not reduce inventory on the other side or create the debit memo. I had the same requirement in a previous project and we used the same process we had for the initial transactions, just everything starts from your plant in Japan and they deliver stock to your plant and charge you.

Question 17: Diagram of SD Customer Master Tables

Can you provide a diagram of SD Customer Master Tables?

A: Here is a diagram of the SD Customer Master Tables.

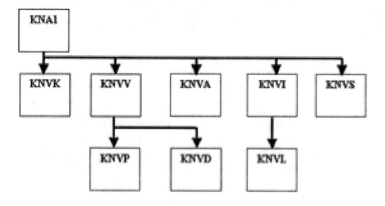

Question 18: Rebate Agreement and Partner Determination

How do I create and process a Rebate agreement?

Why is partner determination so important and also explain the procedure for Partner determination?

A: The following explains how to create a rebate agreement, test it using a sales order and billing it. Then settling it partially or fully using a rebate credit memo. Please use the basic procedure and tweak your IMG settings according to your unique requirements.

Rebate processing:
1. First requirement is that the rebate processing must be active for
a. the customer (check in customer master) ,
b. for the billing type (check in IMG > Billing > rebate processing > active rebate processing > select billing documents for rebate processing.)
c. For the sales organization:
(check in IMG > Billing> rebate processing > active rebate processing > Active rebate processing for sales org.)
2. Next create a rebate agreement for this use T-code VB01. For the rebate agreement type you can choose either 0001 (group rebate) or 0002 material rebate or 0003 (customer rebate), etc.
b. Enter your rebate conditions. Don't forget to enter the accrual rate here.
3. Now test your rebate functionality: create a sales order for the particular customer, sales org (ensure that the billing type used in your sales order is relevant for rebate). Create outbound delivery, transfer order to do picking and post goods issue.
4. Now go to transaction code VB03 and check your rebate by choosing conditions, selecting the condition line and choosing payment data. You will see that the accruals and business volume are updated when accounting doc is created for billing.
5. Settling your rebates:
Once your rebates have been accrued you need to settle the rebate.   For this first release the rebate for settlement by using transaction code VB02. As a trial basis choose B (you can choose

other settings based on your requirement) and choose Create manual accrual. Now enter the amount to be paid and save the rebate agreement.

6. Next display your rebate agreement using Transaction code VB03. Enter your rebate agreement number. Next choose rebate payments > Rebate documents and select partial settlement. Click on the choose button to note down your credit request number.

7. Use transaction code VA02 and release the billing block for your credit request. (Use item overview tab)

8. Now use VF01 to create a rebate credit memo by entering the credit memo request number and save it

9. Now release the credit memo to accounting using vf02.

Question 19: Document Flow in Sales

How are sales documents processed? Can you describe their processes or flow?

A: The sales documents you create are individual documents but they can also form part of a chain of inter-related documents. For example, you may record a customer's telephone inquiry in the system. The customer will then request a quotation, which you then create by referring to the inquiry. The customer later places an order on the basis of the quotation and you create a sales order with reference to the quotation. You ship the goods and bill the customer. After delivery of the goods, the customer claims credit for some damaged goods and you create a free-of-charge delivery with reference to the sales order. The entire chain of documents – the inquiry, the quotation, the sales order, the delivery, the invoice, and the subsequent delivery free of charge – creates a document flow or history. The flow of data from one document into another reduces manual activity and makes problem resolution easier. Inquiry and quotation management in the Sales Information System help you to plan and control your sales.

Question 20: Data flow diagram for shipping and billing

Can you provide a data flow diagram for shipping and billing?

A: The following graphic shows how the various types of sales documents are inter-related and how data subsequently flows into shipping and billing documents.

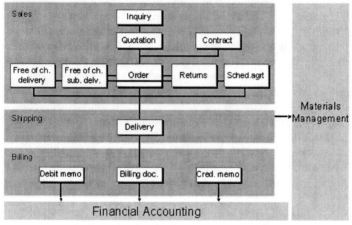

Transaction Code Listing

1. VS00 - Master data
2. VC00 - Sales Support
3. VA00 - Sales
4. VL00 - Shipping
5. VT00 - Transportation
6. VF00 - Billing

Others as follows:
At Configuration:
1. VOV8 - Define Sales documents type (header)
2. OVAZ - Assigning Sales area to sales documents type
3. OVAU - Order reasons
4. VOV4 - Assign Item categories (Item category determination)
5. VOV6 - Schedule line categories
6. OVAL - To assign blocks to relevant sales documents type
7. OVLK - Define delivery types
8. V/06 - Pricing
9. V/08 - Maintain pricing procedure
10. OVKP - Pricing proc determination
11. V/07 - Access sequence

End user:
1. Customer Master Creation-VD01 and XD01 (for full including company code)
   VD02 - Change Customer
   VD03 - Display Customer
   VD04 - Customer Account Changes
   VD06 - Flag for Deletion Customer
   XD01 - Create Customer
   XD02 - Modify Customer
   XD03 - Display Customer
2. Create Other material ----MM00
3. VB11- To create material determination condition record
4. CO09- Material availability Overview
5. VL01 - Create outbound delivery with ref sales order
6. VL04 - Collective processing of delivery
7. VA11 - Create Inquiry
   VA12 - Change Inquiry
   VA13 - Display Inquiry

Sales & Distribution
Sales order / Quote / Scheduling Agreement /Contract

· VA01 - Create Order
· VA02 - Change Order
· VA03 - Display Order
· VA02 - Sales order change
· VA05 - List of sales orders
· VA32 - Scheduling agreement change
· VA42 - Contract change
· VA21 - Create Quotation
· VA22 - Change Quotation
· VA23 - Display Quotation

Billing

· VF02 - Change billing document
· VF11 - Cancel Billing document
· VF04 - Billing due list
· FBL5N - Display Customer invoices by line
· FBL1N - Display Vendor invoices by line

Delivery

· VL02N - Change delivery document
· VL04 - Delivery due list
· VKM5 - List of deliveries
· VL06G - List of outbound deliveries for goods issue
· VL06P - List of outbound deliveries for picking
· VL09 - Cancel goods issue
· VT02N - Change shipment
· VT70 - Output for shipments

General

· VKM3, VKM4 - List of sales documents
· VKM1 - List of blocked SD documents
· VD52 - Material Determination

Most Important Tables

KONV	Conditions for Transaction Data
KONP	Conditions for Items
LIKP	Delivery Header Data
LIPS	Delivery: Item data
VBAK	Sales Document: Header Data
VBAP	Sales Document: Item Data
VBBE	Sales Requirements: Individual Records
VBEH	Schedule line history
VBEP	Sales Document: Schedule Line Data
VBFA	Sales Document Flow
VBLB	Sales document: Release order data
VBLK	SD Document: Delivery Note Header
VBPA	Sales Document: Partner
VBRK	Billing: Header Data
VBRP	Billing: Item Data
VBUK	Sales Document: Header Status and Administrative Data
VBUP	Sales Document: Item Status
VEKP	Handling Unit - Header Table
VEPO	Packing: Handling Unit Item (Contents)
VEPVG	Delivery Due Index

SAP R/3 Netweaver Transaction Codes: Installation, Authorization, and Connection Issues

Question 01: Business Transaction Codes

I was using 'we19' to test an inbound IDoc mbgmcro2. I got the message "status 51 qty and/or delivery completed ind or final issue ind are missing". I have the quantity filled in. I need the delivery completed "ind" or final issue "ind" filled in.

On the e1BP2017_gm_code, I use a code 02.

Can you give me the rundown on the valid codes to use here and what they mean?

A: Here is a list of Business Transactions/Events codes.

- GM_Code 01: Goods receipt for purchase order
- GM_Code 02: Goods receipt for production order
- GM_Code 03: Goods issue
- GM_Code 04: Transfer posting
- GM_Code 05: Other goods receipts
- GM_Code 06: Reversal of goods movements
- GM_Code 07: Subsequent adjustment to a subcontract order

For more details and examples, visit this link:

http://ifr.sap.com/catalog/query.asp?namespace=urn:sap-com:ifr:LO:470X200&type=bapi&name=GoodsMovement.CreateFromData

Question 02: Problems while deploying Java Proxy

We generated Java proxy of our interface and tried to deploy the same into our WAS 6.4 using NetWeaver Dev Studio.

We successfully created ".ear" file. But while deploying the file, it gave the following error:

************************Error************************
Cannot determine sdm host (is empty). Please configure your engine/sdm correctly!

***********************End**********************

The J2EE engine of XI server is configured with NWDS. Also according to the documentation of SAP, we manually restarted the SDM using 'startserver.bat' but still the problem persists.

Can you help us solve this problem?

A: Yes. Make sure that you have given message to the server port (3600) and not to the J2EE port (50000).

Instead of NWDS use SDM directly and deploy the ".ear". The ".ear" file will be there in your workspace folder when you need to use it. In your XI server, search for "RemoteGui.bat", then double click on it click on deployment, then choose your ".ear", then deploy.

Question 03: 'functiontemplate' from repository was <null>

We have a simple R/3 (RFC) to XI to R/3 (RFC) scenario that is currently working. After some time we decided to add another RFC, so we made the necessary work in IR and ID under the existing namespace and scenario respectively. We created the RFCs in every backend doing just the same steps that we did for the existing RFCs that are currently working.

When we sent the message using the new RFCs in SXMB_MONI, we encountered the error:

"com.sap.aii.af.ra.ms.api.DeliveryException: error while processing message to remote system:com.sap.aii.af.rfc.core.client.RfcClientException: functiontemplate from repository was <null>"

We tried to send the payload in the RWB and comparing the new RFC with the one that is working in SXMB_MONI. The difference is that the new RFC shows no response. It just appears in the payload of the receiver but no acknowledgment is shown. On the contrary, the RFC that is working shows acknowledgment:

"Legacy system to which acknowledgment message is to be sent is missing in hoplist (with wasread=false)";

So far, this is the only difference that we have noticed. We have checked the Interface Mappings and Message Mappings and everything looks like the RFCs that work.

We have shutdown java and repeated the steps re-importing the RFCs even with other names, and the error is the same.

Can you help us solve this?

A: Yes. You need to only check your RFC Communication Channel. Make sure it is working correctly.

Question 04: ExchangeProfile Problem

I installed NW04 (ABAP+J2EE) and XI. On page 33 of XI post installation, I created a user XISUPER in ABAP system and rebooted J2EE Server.

I did not find the XISUPER in the J2EE instance. Did I do something wrong here or is there any additional steps needed to be done apart from what document says? As a result, I was not able to do an import of Exchange Profile. I search Google and SDN and found that I could use J2EE_ADMIN, but when I tried that I got the error "You are not authorized to view the requested resource".

My J2ee_admin has Administrator role and for group I have Authenticated Users, Everyone, SAP_J2EE_ADMIN.

Can you give any solution/s to this problem?

A: Two things are important for J2EE users in regards to XI.

1. During installation of J2EE you should select the XI UME option; otherwise users are stored separately in ABAP and J2EE.
2. The UME client must be the correct one as described on page 16 in the XI Install guide.

Reinstall the java system. At the point where it asks for production client, the value should match with the client which you want to use as an Integration server. 000 is the original value; you should match it with the client's. For example, if you called the client 100, then production client should also be 100. Any mismatch will result into the problem you are facing.

Question 05: XI Installation Problems

Our XI installation failed during the phase deploying
SAPXIAF04_1.SCA. The displayed error message in SDM:

Jul 14, 2006 12:35:07... Error: Aborted: development component
'com.sap.aii.adapter.jms.app'/'sap.com'/'SAP
AG'/'7.0004.20050713150837.0000':
Caught exception while checking the login credentials for SAP J2EE
Engine. Check whether the SAP J2EE Engine is up and running.
com.sap.engine.deploy.manager.DeployManagerException: ERROR:
Cannot connect to Host: [cixid] with user name: [J2EE_ADMIN]
Check your login information.
Exception is:
com.sap.engine.services.jndi.persistent.exceptions.NamingException:
Exception while trying to get InitialContext. [Root exception is
com.sap.engine.services.security.exceptions.BaseLoginException:
Cannot create new RemoteLoginContext instance.]
(message ID:
com.sap.sdm.serverext.servertype.inqmy.extern.EngineApplOnlineDepl
oyerImpl.checkLoginCredentials.DMEXC)

I have checked the login name and password is ok. There is an
OSS note 756084 section 4 suggesting the problem was due to
TicketLoginModule. I don't think we have changed any login
modules as it is an installation. We also couldn't start the VA.

Do you have any suggestion or solution for this problem?

A: You can solve the problem by doing the following:

Configtool -> dispatcher -> Service -> P4.

For 'bindhost' option, you will need to enter your CI instance
hostname/ipaddress (default is 0.0.0.0).

Question 06: XI Install Error

I was attempting to install XI on a MSCS cluster Environment - Windows Server 2003 Enterprise Edition, running Oracle 9.2.0.6. I have installed our Dev, QA and Production systems successfully. I also installed Oracle, OraFS, ABAP+Java on MSCS Cluster, and was trying to install XI Component.

When SAP installer was running, I got the following error message after I have entered the Domain, userid and password:

INFO 2006-03-08 15:46:29
Installation start: Wednesday, 08 March 2006, 15:46:25; installation directory: C:\sapinstall\XI; product to be installed: SAP NetWeaver '04 Support Release 1> NetWeaver Components Running on Java> XI Components>
Exchange Infrastructure Installation

WARNING 2006-03-08 15:46:46
The step storeSidadmPassword with step key
ExchangeInfrastructure|ind|ind|ind|ind|ind|0|Gener
icAskJavahomeAndPasswords|ind|ind|ind|ind|ind|0|st
oreSidadmPassword was executed with status
ERROR.

WARNING 2006-03-08 15:46:52
An error occurred during the installation.

The password for <SID>adm has the "@" sign in, and I wonder if this caused the error.

Is there a solution for this?

A: Yes. You need to do the following.

In the control.xml, change the line:

WindowsDomain = gui.getInputValue("fld_WindowsDomain");
To
WindowsDomain = context.get("WindowsDomain");
Continue installation.

Question 07: FTP Connection Error

I tried to run the File to IDoc scenario. In this case I used FTP as sender channel. During execution in the adapter monitor I got the following error:

Sender Adapter v1028 for Party '', Service 'FILE_BS':
Configured at 12:45:07 2006-07-06
Processing Error: Error connecting to ftp server '192.168.13.9':
com.sap.aii.adapter.file.ftp.FTPEx: /Inetpub/ftproot: The system cannot find the path specified.
last retry interval started 12:45:07 2006-07-06
length 60,000 secs

Can you tell me what caused the error?

I did all configuration everywhere and I have given everyone permission. I kept the directory in a shared folder. I am able to access the directory from XI server.

Can you tell if any other configuration is missing?

Folder path : /Inetpub/ftproot
file name : xiinput.txt

A: You need to first do a cross check on the path >> Folder path : /Inetpub/ftproot

Then check if you have assigned read/write rights to the FTP folder.

Note that if your ftproot is the FTP folder, then / is your root folder in XI adapter so if you have a folder input in ftproot, in your CC you will specify:

folder : /input

And not:

ftproot/input

Question 08: XI Lost Connection to J2EE

Sometimes, the XI system seems to lose connection to the J2EE server, and the RFC connections AI_DIRECTORY_JCOSERVER, AI_RUNTIME_JCOSERVER, etc. stops working, and then all messages fail.

Logs in dev_jcontrol show errors like:

[Thr 3596] Thu Sep 15 18:34:24 2005
[Thr 3596] ***LOG Q0I=> NiPRead: recv (10054: WSAECONNRESET: Connection reset by peer) [ninti.c 785]
[Thr 3596] *** ERROR => MsINiRead: NiBufReceive failed (NIECONN_BROKEN) [msxxi.c 2488]
[Thr 3596] *** ERROR => MsIReadFromHdl: NiRead (rc=NIECONN_BROKEN) [msxxi.c 1652]
[Thr 3596] ***LOG Q0I=> NiPConnect2: SiPeekPendConn (10065: WSAEHOSTUNREACH: No route to host) [nixxi_r.cpp 8605]
[Thr 3596] *** ERROR => MsIAttachEx: NiBufConnect to sapserver4/3601 failed (rc=NIECONN_REFUSED) [msxxi.c 633]
[Thr 3596] *** WARNING => Can't reconnect to message server (sapserver4/3601) [rc = -100]-> reconnect [jcntrms.c 296]
[Thr 6612] ***LOG Q0I=> NiPRead: recv (10054: WSAECONNRESET: Connection reset by peer) [ninti.c 785]

[Thr 3596] Thu Sep 15 18:34:29 2005
[Thr 3596] *** ERROR => MsIAttachEx: NiBufConnect to sapserver4/3601 failed (rc=NIECONN_REFUSED) [msxxi.c 633]
[Thr 3596] *** WARNING => Can't reconnect to message server (sapserver4/3601) [rc = -100]-> reconnect [jcntrms.c 296]

Do you have any suggestions concerning this problem?

A: I see this issue often in our XI systems. To date, there is only one solution: restart the JCos. We have not been able to determine why these JCos lose their registration in the gateway, but they do.

The next time it happens, go to tcode SMGW and go to "Logged on clients". You should see the above mentioned RFC's logged onto the gateway. If you don't then open the VA on the XI server to stop then start each affected JCo. Once it is restarted, check the gateway again to see if they have registered. Your system will be good to go without restarting the entire J2EE engine.

Question 09: JCo Connection Parameters and Migration through Dev/QA/Prod

I know how to open up from within XI a JCo connection to an SAP client.

How do you determine what SAP client to connect to and how to migrate that along when you move the XI development from Dev to QA to Prod?

A: You will need to manage with a "prop file". Just give it the same name on the three systems (Dev, QA, and Production). Keep it in a separate 'Imported Archive' (separate java package as well), and load it from java as resource. You can do this in 1 SWCV and then have others base themselves off of that one so you only have to do it once.

If you cannot upload objects directly into QA and Production, a "prop file" on the "filesystem" is better. Choose a suitable location existing on the three systems.

When using the Lookup API with RFC/JCo, you still need the name of the "Service without Pary". You have to put this name in a properties file on the "filesystem" of the XI server. The file will have the same name (but different contents) on Dev, QA and Production.

You can also use the SAP XI value mapping to store configuration parameters in.

Question 10: sm58 - Name or Password is Incorrect

I have encountered a problem. After the configuration of an IDoc to File, I am facing an error "sm58" after successfully sending an IDoc with "we19".

Status text indicated: "Name or password is incorrect. Please re-enter".

After retrying, I've got a new error message:

"User is locked. Please notify the person responsible".

How do I sort this out?

A: You need to check your SM59 connection (Target system column in SM58). There is most probably a userid/password defined that is incorrect. You have to unlock the user in the target system.

Be careful. Normally, when you try to access your SAP systems with an invalid user id / password more than 3 times, the user gets locked. You will have to ask your admin to unlock the user and then make your remote log on test in Sm 59.

Cross check first with these steps in what you have done so far.

While doing an IDoc to XI to File scenario, the points to take note of are as follows:

1. You don't need a DT, MT or a message interface for the IDoc as it itself acts as the Message Interface.
2. You import the IDoc and use the same in your mapping.
3. In this configuration, note that you don't have a sender agreement as you don't have a sender IDoc adapter.

If it is that you wanted to send an IDoc from XI (File to IDoc), then in this case:

Points 1 and 2 will remain, but the 3rd will not. You will need a sender agreement for the file and a receiver agreement for the IDoc.

IDoc to File scenario reference:

https://www.sdn.sap.com/irj/sdn/weblogs?blog=/pub/wlg/1819

Configurations in R/3 side:

1. SM 59 (RFC destinations)

   Create a RFC destination on the XI server. The connection type should be R/3 connection. The target host needs to be the XI server.

2. WE 21 (Ports in IDoc processing)

   Create a transactional port. Provide the RFC destination created in this.

3. BD 54

   Create a logical system.

4. WE 20 (Partner Profiles)

   a. Create a new partner profile under partner type LS.

   b. Assign the message type in outbound parameters.

   c. Open the message type (Dbl click) and configure the receiver port to the port created.

XI Server Configurations:

1. SM59 (RFC destination)

   Configure the RFC destination specific to the R/3 system.

2. IDX1 (Port maintenance in IDoc Adapter)

Create a port and provide the RFC destination.

TESTING:

WE19 for pushing the IDoc in XI through trfc port.

To be able to trigger your IDOC from the SAP ISU system, you will have to set the partner profile in "we20". Select your Business System (mostly under Logical system) and then create outbound entries for whichever IDoc you want to trigger.

You define your basic type also in your partner profile settings. Please go thru the following links to get a better idea about partner profile:

http://help.sap.com/saphelp_nw04/helpdata/en/dc/6b833243 d711d1893e0000e8323c4f/frameset.htm

http://help.sap.com/saphelp_nw04/helpdata/en/dc/6b7cd343d 711d1893e0000e8323c4f/frameset.htm

http://help.sap.com/saphelp_nw04/helpdata/en/32/692037b1f 10709e10000009b38f839/content.htm

http://help.sap.com/saphelp_nw04/helpdata/en/5e/b8f8bf356 dc84096e4fedc2cd71426/frameset.htm

I would suggest that you go through these blogs if anymore issue arises.

https://weblogs.sdn.sap.com/pub/wlg/1439

https://weblogs.sdn.sap.com/pub/wlg/1843

Question 11: Log-in in error

After logging into SXMB_IFR, I tried to get some SLD components but I instead got the "You are not authorized to view the requested resource in SLD".

What do I need to do to get into SLD?

A: You will need to check the role or level of authorization you have.

SAP_SLD_ADMINISTRATOR

Or

SAP_SLD_CONFIGURATOR

Or

SAP_XI_CONFIGURATOR

Or

SAP_XI_CONTENT_ORGANIZER

For a complete definition of roles and level of authorization, check out the following link.

http://help.sap.com/saphelp_nw04/helpdata/en/c4/51104159e cef23e10000000a155106/content.htm

Question 12: RWB Error during Message Monitoring

I got the following error during Message monitoring:

"User XIRWBUSER has no RFC authorization for function group HTTPTREE, error key: RFC_ERROR_SYSTEM_FAILURE"

What can this mean and how do I fix it?

A: First, check if your XIRWBUSER has its standard roles.

SAP_XI_RWB_SERV_USER
SAP_XI_RWB_SERV_USER_MAIN

Normally the mentioned roles should be sufficient.

Another key is the SP level of your XI system. After a new SP level, XI will request more authorizations which have not been included in the standard role so far. You will need to open up an OSS message at SAP.

The standard role has been extended with a new SP but the according profile has not been regenerated, so you will also need to carry out a mass generation of all profiles for SAP_XI roles and after that a user comparison.

Question 13: Websphere MQ Problem

I have a problem with Websphere MQ Sender adapter. I know that in the queue are messages but XI doesn't get them. I have checked everything in the adapter engine and integration engine.

There are no errors and all lights are green. There is no payload.

How do I make the adapter work?

A: Yes. You need to reset your communication channel. Deactivate and activate it again.

Question 14: Reassigning Change List to a Different User

One user in our system has changed SWCV, but did not activate the change list. The system pops out the message saying:

"If necessary, you can reassign the other user's change list to yourself"

How do I find what the system requires?

A: Open the Integration Builder Web Start application and go to the "change list" tab. Select the user that has changed the SWCV and press "Display". You can now assign the change list to yours if you right-click on it and press "OK".

Question 15: Setting up HTTPS

We added an SSL certificate to our XI server. We are struggling our way through the documentation for the steps to exchange messages via HTTPS.

How do I set the adapter to use HTTPS in the integration directory?

I only see HTTP 1.0 in the options for protocol while trying to setup the HTTP adapter settings.

The external party is the receiver of messages from us. During testing, no security was in place so we tried sending to a URL using the HTTP adapter. Now, HTTPS protocol must be used. However, for the HTTP adapter type, HTTPS protocol is not a drop down option.

Does that mean I have to use adapter type "XI" to send to a URL via HTTPS?

A: You need to do the following to fix your problem.

In the communication channel select the following:

- Transport protocol : HTTP1.0
- Addressing Type : HTTP Destination
- HTTP Destination: your ABAP RFC (type G)

In your RFC destination, you need to specify the URL and the certificate to use to connect to your server.

Question 16: Unable to Find any Adapter Engines

I tried to execute a scenario. An xml-file is read from a drive by the XI system. XI read the values. Another xml-file containing some parts of this info was written to another location. I saw that the file was read and removed.

However, when I checked the monitoring, I found following error message:

```
<SAP:Error xmlns:SAP="http://sap.com/xi/XI/Message/30"
xmlns:SOAP="http://schemas.xmlsoap.org/soap/envelope/"
SOAP:mustUnderstand="">
<SAP:Category>XIServer</SAP:Category>
<SAP:Code
area="INTERNAL">AE_DETAILS_GET_ERROR</SAP:Code>
<SAP:P1>af.cx1.cernum05\cx1</SAP:P1>
<SAP:P2 />
<SAP:P3 />
<SAP:P4 />
<SAP:AdditionalText>Exception in SLD client:
AbapSLDRequestHandler.exe: Unable to find any Adapter
Engines</SAP:AdditionalText>
<SAP:ApplicationFaultMessage namespace="" />
<SAP:Stack>Error when reading the access data (URL, user,
password) for the Adapter Engine
af.cx1.cernum05\cx1</SAP:Stack>
<SAP:Retry>M</SAP:Retry>
</SAP:Error>
```

Is there some configuration missing? Are there things which I missed to check out?

We are running XI3.0 SP9.

A: You need to execute transaction SE37 and test the function module SAI_AE_DETAILS_GET. Enter your AE_NAME af.<hostname>.<sysid> and execute.

You also need to run an SLDCHECK and check whether your exchange profile parameter checks are successful. The last one calling function is EXCHANGE_PROFILE_GET_PARAMETER.

If these are correct, check that your com.sap.aii.adapterframework.serviceuser.name and com.sap.aii.adapterframework.serviceuser.pwd are correct.

If these are correct, check whether the user id is locked.

Also check whether you are using the SLD which is on your XI server or you are pointing to a different SLD.

Question 17: Setting the Username & Password for the Plain HTTP Adapter

When I passed in a HTTP request into the integration engine's plain_http adapter url, I was required to give a username and a password for authentication.

Is it possible to set this username and password globally somewhere?

This is to avoid the username and password to be given again and again for each message. The requirement is like all http messages from our partners will be routed through a proxy in the DMZ which would have an authentication and we do not want the XI user credentials to be given again repeatedly.

A: You need to use SICF, then sap/xi/adapter_plain, then change button. Enter client, username, password, and language.

If you want to just test the http adapter use this code:

```
<html>

<script type="text/javascript">;
<!--
function button1_onclick() {
var result = "Result: ";
var payload = "<?xml version=\"1.0\" encoding=\"UTF-8\" ?>";
// escape "http://"
var senderNamespace =
escape(document.MessageParameters.SenderNamespace.value);

var reqString = "http://"
reqString = reqString +
document.MessageParameters.Server.value+":";
reqString = reqString +
document.MessageParameters.Port.value +
"/sap/xi/adapter_plain?";
reqString = reqString + "namespace=" + senderNamespace;
reqString = reqString + "&interface=" +
document.MessageParameters.SenderInterface.value;
```

```
reqString = reqString + "&service=" +
document.MessageParameters.SenderService.value;
reqString = reqString + "&party=" +
document.MessageParameters.SenderParty.value;
reqString = reqString + "&agency=" +
document.MessageParameters.SenderAgency.value;
reqString = reqString + "&scheme=" +
document.MessageParameters.SenderScheme.value;
reqString = reqString + "&QOS=" +
document.MessageParameters.qos.value;

reqString = reqString + "&queueid=httpclient";

reqString = reqString + "&sap-user=" +
document.MessageParameters.username.value;
reqString = reqString + "&sap-password=" +
document.MessageParameters.password.value;
reqString = reqString + "&sap-client=" +
document.MessageParameters.Client.value
reqString = reqString + "&sap-language=EN";
var xhttp = new ActiveXObject("msxml2.xmlhttp");

for (var i=0; i<document.MessageParameters.retry.value; i++) {

  xhttp.open ("POST", reqString, false);
  document.MessageParameters.URL.value=reqString;

  if (document.MessageParameters.Source[0].checked == true) {
    payload = "<?xml version=\"1.0\" encoding=\"UTF-8\" ?> "+
document.MessageParameters.xmlData.value;
    xhttp.send (payload);
  } else{
    var xmlDoc = new ActiveXObject("microsoft.xmldom");
    xmlDoc.async=false;
    xmlDoc.load (document.MessageParameters.xmlFile.value);
    xhttp.send (xmlDoc);
  }
  result = result + "\nhttp-Status: " + xhttp.status + " " +
xhttp.statusText + " \nPayload:\n" + xhttp.responseText;

  xhttp.close;
  document.MessageParameters.response.value=result;
}
```

```
}
//-->
</script>
<head></head>

<body>

<h3>Client Http Adapter </h3>
<form name="MessageParameters">
<table border="1" cellpadding="0" cellspacing="0"
style="border-collapse: collapse" bordercolor="#111111"
width="100%">
<h4>Header</h4>
<tbody>
<tr>
<td width="10%"><label>Server Host</label> </td>
<td width="22%">

<!-- Change server and port here -->

<input type="text" id="host" name="Server"
value="YourServer" size="20" /> </td>
<td width="10%"><label>Server Port</label> </td>
<td width="22%"><input type="text" id="port" name="Port"
value="8000" size="10" /> </td>
</tr>
<tr>
<td width="10%">Client</td>
<td width="22%">

<!-- Change client here -->

<input type="text" id="client" name="Client"
value="100" size="3" /></td>
<td width="10%"> </td>
<td width="22%"> </td>
</tr>
<tr>
<td width="10%"><label>Sender Service</label> </td>
<td width="22%">

<!-- Change sender service here -->

<input type="text" id="senderService"
```

```
name="SenderService" value="TravelAgencyCS" size="40" />
</td>
<td width="10%">Quality of Service</td>
<td width="22%">
    <select size="1" name="qos">
    <option value="BE">Best Effort (synchronous)</option>
    <option value="EO" selected>Exactly Once
(asynchronous)</option>
    <option value="EOIO">Exactly Once in Order</option>
    </select>
</td>
</tr>
<tr>
<td width="10%"><label>Sender Interface</label> </td>

<!-- Change sender interface name here -->

<td width="22%"><input type="text" id="senderInterface"
name="SenderInterface" value="BookingOrdersOut" size="40"
/> </td>
<td width="10%"><label>Sender Namespace</label> </td>
<td width="22%">

<!-- Change sender interface namespace  here -->

<input type="text" id="senderNamespace"
name="SenderNamespace"
value="http://sap.com/xi/rkt/CaseStudy/group99"
size="40" /></td>
</tr>
</tbody>
</table>
<br>
<table border="1" cellpadding="0" cellspacing="0"
style="border-collapse: collapse" bordercolor="#111111"
width="100%">
<h4>Optional Parameters</h4>
<tbody>
<tr>
<td width="10%">Sender Party</td>
<td width="22%"><input type="text" id="senderParty"
name="SenderParty" size="40" /></td>
</tr>
<tr>
```

```html
<td width="10%">Sender Agency</td>
<td width="22%"><input type="text" id="senderAgency"
name="SenderAgency" size="40" /></td>
<td width="10%">Sender Scheme</td>
<td width="22%"><input type="text" id="senderScheme"
name="SenderScheme" size="40" /></td>
</tr>

<TR>
  <TD width="10%">Username</TD>

<!-- Change user name here -->

  <TD width="22%"><INPUT id=username size=40
value=xiappluser name=username></TD>
  <TD width="10%">Password</TD>
  <TD width="22%"><INPUT id=password type=password
size=40  name=password></TD></TR>
 <TR>
  <TD width="10%">Retry</TD>
  <TD width="22%"><INPUT id=retry type=number size=40
value=1 name=retry></TD>
 </TR>

</tbody>
</table>
<br>
<table border="1" cellpadding="0" cellspacing="0"
style="border-collapse: collapse" bordercolor="#111111"
width="100%">
<h4>Payload</h4>
<tbody>
<tr>
<fieldset style="padding: 2">
<td width="50%"><input type="radio" name="Source"
value="Textarea" checked="checked" />Type in XML</td>
<td width="50%"><input type="radio" name="Source"
value="File" />Upload File</td>
</fieldset>
</tr>
<tr>
<td width="50%"><textarea name="xmlData" rows="10"
cols="60">&lt;a&gt;test&lt;/a&gt;</textarea></td>
<td width="50%"><input type="file" name="xmlFile" size="40"
```

```
/> </td>
</tr>
</tbody>
</table>
<p>
<input type="button" value="Send" id="button1"
name="button1" LANGUAGE="javascript"
onclick="button1_onclick()" />
</p>
<hr />
<table border="1" cellpadding="0" cellspacing="0"
style="border-collapse: collapse" bordercolor="#111111"
width="100%">
<h4>Result</h4>
  <P align=left>URL: <TEXTAREA name=URL
cols=104></TEXTAREA></P>
  <P align=left> </P>
<tbody>
<tr>
<td width="50%"><textarea name="response" rows="5"
cols="60"></textarea></td>
</tr>
</tbody>
</table>
</form>

</body>

</html>
```

The code is now updated to allow multiple messages and for new input fields for User and Password.

This HTML code was originally introduced by Joachim Orb for educational purposes.

You can find a description here:

https://www.sdn.sap.com/irj/servlet/prt/portal/prtroot/docs/li
brary/uuid/66dadc6e-0a01-0010-9ea9-bb6d8ca48cc8

I recommend that you overwrite the required parameters direct in the HTML source.

Question 18: Outbound File Adapter

I am trying to create an outbound file adapter, designed to receive XML messages from XI Integration engine and store it in a file.

Reading from the document "Configuring the Receiver File/FTP Adapter",

http://help.sap.com/saphelp_nw04/helpdata/en/bc/bb79d6061007419a081e58cbeaaf28/content.htm

I believe that configuration should look like this:

```
---------------------------------------
## file adapter java class
classname=com.sap.aii.messaging.adapter.ModuleXMB2FILE
version=30

mode=XMB2FILE

##Bind the address for Integration port to connect to
XI.httpPort=1981
XI.httpService=/TempFileTran

file.TargetFilename=mindichFile.txt
file.writeMode=overwrite
---------------------------------------
```

The response I receive is "version not set" and adapter does not start running.

Is there a way to correct this? I use a XI 2.0 SR1.

A: The configuration "version=30" has to be removed. It is not needed in the file adapter.

Although the documentation specifically mentions the fact that "version=30" must exists, it is version dependent.

If you use J2SE adapters to connect with XI3, you may need to put the version configuration.

Question 19: J2SE Adapter Registration

I tried using SLD Access service on J2SE adapter but it does not work. This J2SE Adapter Engine is registered in the SLD. My J2SE adapter was never available in the configuration means; in the communication channel ex: file adapter, the adapter engine drop down and all I have is the Integration Server. My J2SE adapter was never listed there.

How do you register J2SE adapter with XI?

A: First, see page 10 of "SAP XI Release 3.0 SR1" installation guide.

http://help.sap.com/bp_bpmv130/Documentation/Installation/XI30InstallGuide.pdf#search=%22SAP%20XI%20SR1%20installation%20guide%22

It mentions the disadvantage of just plain J2SE adapter engine as "Less integration into the SAP XI environment due to lack of central configuration and monitoring services".

It makes sense because in SLD you can only create technical/business system as Web AS Java (say for J2EE decentralized adapter engine) and not as J2SE adapter engine.

But if you want a receiver file adapter, you need to maintain in the adapter configuration:

XI.httpPort=<port_no>
XI.httpService=<service>

Then in the communication channel, you choose XI protocol (XI 3.0) and as URL you enter:

http://<J2SE-host>:<port_no>/<service>

eg:

XI.httpPort=1234

XI.httpService=/file/Receiver

-> http://<J2SE-host>:1234/file/Receiver

The file adapter business system needs to be created in SLD to which you will send the message using XML protocol (XI Adapter). The standalone adapter in the business system will then do the XMB2File conversion.

Question 20: Problem with SOAP adapter

I have configured the SOAP adapter to send a message through to a WS-I compliant web service.

I got the following error message:

```
<?xml version="1.0" encoding="UTF-8" standalone="yes" ?>
- <!-- Call Adapter
-->
- <SAP:Error xmlns:SAP="http://sap.com/xi/XI/Message/30"
xmlns:SOAP="http://schemas.xmlsoap.org/soap/envelope/"
SOAP:mustUnderstand="1">
<SAP:Category>XIAdapter</SAP:Category>
<SAP:Code
area="PARSING">ADAPTER.SOAP_EXCEPTION</SAP:Code>
<SAP:P1 />
<SAP:P2 />
<SAP:P3 />
<SAP:P4 />
<SAP:AdditionalText>soap fault: Server did not recognize the
value of HTTP Header SOAPAction: .</SAP:AdditionalText>
<SAP:ApplicationFaultMessage namespace="" />
<SAP:Stack />
<SAP:Retry>M</SAP:Retry>
</SAP:Error>
```

Can you point me to the right direction?

A: Your server requires a SOAP-Action.

If you have a WSDL for the message, look at the attributesoapAction of the tag soap:operation. Take the parameter there and type the value in the SOAP adapter receiver channel configuration.

Question 21: RFC Adapter as Sender

We have a business scenario wherein I have to execute the RFC function (asynchronous) from an ABAP in R/3 and update the data in DB2 tables (asynchronous).

I used RFC as sender (asynchronous) and JDBC as receiver (asynchronous). I configured/registered the RFC connection in SM59 and used the same program id in RFC sender adapter. I tested the connection in standalone mode and it is working.

The RFC function, when I imported, will have a request and a response. The data that I require to send to JDBC adapter is in the response. I tried to use RFC response and created a message interface. Then I used that in my interface mapping and also in the sender & receiver agreements. In the message mapping I used, response was imported.

I got an error message "sender agreement not found". I changed the sender agreement to use RFC function as sender interface, but I cannot use this function module for my mapping, as it does not contain the response.

I deleted the sender/receiver agreements and receiver/interface determination. Then I started creating a new interface determination but I can't find the interface mapping as the interface mapping user response.

In my business scenario I need a user interface before calling the RFC function. I wrote a wrapper around the RFC which will provide me with user interface; then I would like to send the response data to XI using RFC sender.

We are on XI3.0 SP13. I have to use the response of the RFC in the message mapping. It should be able to send the data to JDBC Adapter.

How do I fix this?

A: If you want to capture the response of an RFC execution in XI and then map this response to another structure (in your case a JDBC structure) inside XI message mapping, then you will have to use the RFC receiver adapter of XI and NOT the RFC sender adapter. If you use the RFC sender adapter, it means that your SAP system is acting as an RFC CLIENT. What happens is the REQUEST structure in your RFC destination will be converted to RFC-XML by the RFC sender adapter of XI and is available for further processing.

If you want to send the RESPONSE structure of an RFC to XI , one way is to execute the RFC in SAP (without passing this thru XI). Now you have to pass the result of this RFC execution to XI by assigning it to a request structure of another RFC in your ABAP code and pass it to XI using RFC sender adapter. If not , you can use a dummy RFC in SAP to send a trigger to XI, execute the actual RFC in XI using RFC receiver adapter, capture the response, map it to your JDBC structure and you are done.

Check out these threads for additional reference:

https://forums.sdn.sap.com/thread.jspa?forumID=44&threadID=39026&messageID=378929#378929

https://forums.sdn.sap.com/thread.jspa?forumID=44&threadID=57874&messageID=607693#607693

https://forums.sdn.sap.com/thread.jspa?forumID=44&threadID=33356&messageID=313604#313604

Question 22: "No steps" Mapping & Determination in Pipeline (SXMB_MONI)

I'm using a SAP/R3 IDoc->XI->IDoc SAP/R3 with IDoc RSINFO. All is fine and works well.

But in SXMB_MONI, I don't see pipeline steps:

- Receiver determination
- Interface determination

I only see:

- Inbound message (central)
- Receiver grouping
- Response

Is there any way of customizing to log and see those steps?

A: To specifically see all the logging desired in SXMB_MONI, use SXMB_ADM and set the following flags to "1";

category/parameter
RUNTIME/LOGGING
RUNTIME/LOGGING_PROPAGATION
RUNTIME/LOGGING_SYNC

These logging parameters should be set only on DEV systems, as they will introduce additional disk space requirement.

Check this blog for additional information.

https://weblogs.sdn.sap.com/pub/wlg/1629

Question 23: Mapping Flat Structure in Complex Structure

Is it possible to use graphical mapping to obtain the following result?

I have this example input message type:

```xml
<?xml version="1.0" encoding="UTF-8"?>
<nso:MT_CONFERMA xmlns:nso="http://prova">
<HEADER>
<TRASM>1</TRASM>
<MDI>1234</MDI>
</HEADER>
<HEADER>
<TRASM>2</TRASM>
<MDI>2657</MDI>
</HEADER>
<ROW>
<TRASM>1</TRASM>
<RNUM>1.1</RNUM>
<ART>1.1</ART>
</ROW>
<ROW>
<TRASM>1</TRASM>
<RNUM>1.2</RNUM>
<ART>1.2</ART>
</ROW>
<ROW>
<TRASM>2</TRASM>
<RNUM>2.1</RNUM>
<ART>2.1</ART>
</ROW>
<ROW>
<TRASM>2</TRASM>
<RNUM>2.2</RNUM>
<ART>2.2</ART>
</ROW>
</nso:MT_CONFERMA>
```

Result:

```
<ns0:MT_OUT xmlns:ns0="http://prova">
<DATA>
<TRASM>1</TRASM>
<MDI>1234</MDI>
<ROW>
<TRASM>1</TRASM>
<RNUM>1.1</RNUM>
<ART>1.1</ART>
</ROW>
<ROW>
<TRASM>1</TRASM>
<RNUM>1.2</RNUM>
<ART>1.2</ART>
</ROW>
</DATA>
<DATA>
<TRASM>2</TRASM>
<MDI>2657</MDI>
<ROW>
<TRASM>2</TRASM>
<RNUM>2.1</RNUM>
<ART>2.1</ART>
</ROW>
<ROW>
<TRASM>2</TRASM>
<RNUM>2.2</RNUM>
<ART>2.2</ART>
</ROW>
</DATA>
</ns0:MT_OUT>
```

The split data is "TRASM". I tried some methods but without the correct solution.

Can you help me solve this?

A: Yes. Apply this correction:

CONFERMA - > MT_OUT
HEADER -> DATA
TRASM - >TRASM
MDI - >MDI

ROW:

TRASM (cont. CONFERMA)- >split(byvalue-value change)ROW
RNUM- >RNUM
ART->ART

Question 24: RFC Sender Problem (Asynchronous)

Is there a way to detect from a RFC FM asynchronous call if XI is down?

I understand that if the RFC call is asynchronous, no exceptions are caught. But is there a workaround on catching the error?

A: You can use transaction SM58 to restart LUW on your source system. In this transaction you will see all errors in asynchronous RFC communication.

Acknowledgements and references for FICO /SD Tcodes:

http://en.wikipedia.org

https://www.sdn.sap.com

http://tech.groups.yahoo.com

http://www.thespot4sap.com

Duke University Online SAP Guide:

http://r3.duke.edu/stepbystep/index.html

Index

Printed in the United States
99682LV00002B/186/A